D0858238

Medieval

Studies

Library

Donated by *Michael P. McHugh*

THE ALPHA CLASSICS

General Editor: R. C. CARRINGTON, M.A., D.Phil.

CAESAR'S GALLIC WAR, BOOK I, edited by C. Ewan, M.A.

CAESAR'S INVASIONS OF BRITAIN, edited by R. C. Carrington, M.A., D.Phil.

CAESAR'S GALLIC WAR, BOOK V, edited by R. C. Carrington, M.A., D.Phil.

CICERO ON HIMSELF, selections from Cicero chosen and edited by N. Fullwood, B.A.

CICERO'S SPEECHES FOR MARCELLUS AND LIGARIUS, edited by James Paterson, M.A.

CORNELIUS NEPOS: THREE LIVES—ALCIBIADES, DION, ATTICUS, edited by R. Roebuck, M.A.

ERASMUS AND HIS TIMES, a selection from the Letters of Erasmus and his circle, edited by G. S. Facer, B.A.

EURIPIDES' HECUBA, edited by F. W. King, B.A.

HORACE ON HIMSELF, selections from Horace chosen and edited by A. H. Nash-Williams, M.A.

LIVY: BOOK V, edited by J. E. Pickstone, M.A.

LIVY: SCIPIO AFRICANUS, selections from Livy, Books XXVI-XXX, edited by T. A. Buckney, M.A.

LUCRETIUS ON MATTER AND MAN, edited by A. S. Cox, M.A.

MARTIAL AND HIS TIMES, a selection from Martial chosen and edited by K. W. D. Hull.

OVID ON HIMSELF, selections edited by J. A. Harrison, M.A.

OVID'S METAMORPHOSES: AN ANTHOLOGY, edited by J. E. Dunlop, M.A., Ph.D.

PLINY ON HIMSELF, selections from the Letters edited by H. A. B. White, M.A.

VERGIL'S AENEID I, edited by P. G. Hunter, M.A.

VERGIL'S AENEID II, edited by J. E. Dunlop, M.A., Ph.D.

VERGIL'S AENEID III, edited by R. W. Moore, M.A., D.Litt.

VERGIL'S AENEID IX, edited by B. Tilly, M.A., Ph.D.

VERGIL'S AENEID XII, edited by W. F. Gosling, M.A. and J. J. Smith, B.A.

THE THOUGHT OF CICERO, selections from Cicero, edited for more advanced students by S. J. Wilson, B.A.

BEDE'S HISTORIA ECCLESIASTICA, a selection edited for more advanced students by F. W. Garforth, M.A.

G. BELL AND SONS, LTD

YORK HOUSE, PORTUGAL STREET, LONDON, W.C.2

THE ALPHA CLASSICS
General Editor: R. C. CARRINGTON, M.A., D.Phil.
Headmaster of St. Olave's School,
formerly Senior Classical Master, Dulwich College

ERASMUS
AND HIS TIMES

ERASMUS
AND HIS TIMES

A Selection from the Letters of
Erasmus and his Circle

CHOSEN AND EDITED BY

G. S. FACER, B.A.

Assistant, Charterhouse

Property of
Charles A. Owen, Jr.
Medieval Studies Library

LONDON
G. BELL & SONS LTD
1967

First published 1951
Reprinted 1958, 1963,
1967 (*with corrections and additions*)

Printed in Great Britain by
NEILL & CO. LTD., EDINBURGH

PREFACE

TEACHERS as well as pupils are apt to get a little tired of struggling through portions of Caesar, Livy or Cicero, who often seem to be dealing with matters remote from our experience. The letters of Cicero and Pliny give us a clear picture of their authors and the age in which they lived, but many of them are too difficult for forms of about the standard of the ordinary level of the General Certificate.

Erasmus, on the other hand, lived in an exciting age not so far removed from our own, and one with whose history we are reasonably familiar. He met and corresponded with most of the great men of his time, and wrote in a Latin in which Cicero would not have found many serious faults.

In this selection, the occasional irregularities in spelling and syntax have been either amended in the text or pointed out in the notes. Some of the longer letters have been shortened, and portions of two of them are translated.

My aim has been to stress the connection of Erasmus with English history rather than to illustrate his whole life, and to choose letters in which the human interest predominates. Eight letters are written to Erasmus by such men as Colet, More, Fisher and Warham.

The text is that of P. S. Allen's Edition, by kind permission of the Oxford University Press, and I have made grateful use of Froude's *Life and Letters of Erasmus*, and R. W. Chambers' *Life of Thomas More*. Some of the letters, whose choice was inevitable, are also in Allen's *Selection of Erasmus' Letters*, from which I have gained much valuable information. There are many books on Erasmus, but a view of him from an unusual angle is to be found in Van Loon's *Lives*.

The separate introductions to the Letters are mainly historical. A good deal of help in translation has been given in the Notes, though not so much as to avoid the necessity for an intelligent use of the Vocabulary.

G. S. F.

CHARTERHOUSE,
1951.

CONTENTS

LIST OF PLATES

DESIDERIVS ERASMVS ROTTERODAMVS.
Qui Patriæ lumen qui nostri gloria secli
THOMÆ HOWARDO, COMITI ARVNDELIÆ & SVRREIÆ, PRIMO ANGLIÆ COMITI, DOMINO HOWARDO,
MALTRAVERS, MOWBRAY, SEGRAVE, BREVS, CLVN, & OSLÆTRIÆ, COMITI MARESCALLO ANGLIÆ,
NOBILISSIMI PERISCELIDIS SIVE GARTERY ORDINIS EQVITI & SERENISSIMO REGI
CAROLO MAGNÆ BRITANNIÆ FRANCIÆ & HIBERNIÆ REGI AB INTIMIS CONCILYS, *artiumq̃*
omnium liberalium Mecænati maximo, hanc Erasmi effigiē amoris ergo humiliter Lucas
Vorstermañ Sculptor D.D: Hansus Holbenius *pinxit.*   Cum Privilegio Reg.

I. Holbein painted Erasmus many times. This portrait, from a later
engraving, is one of the second series, dated about 1530, when Erasmus
was in his middle sixties. Hans Holbein began his career in Basel,
designing woodcuts for the books published by Froben. Erasmus gave
him letters of introduction to friends in England, and he was the guest
of Thomas More in Chelsea during his first visit (1526–1528).

II. This is from a brief note written by Erasmus within six weeks of his death (*aegra manu*, as he says), to a merchant of Antwerp named Erasmus Schets. It is worth studying as a specimen of the handwriting of the period, since nearly all the letters of the Latin alphabet are to be found in it. Notice the many abbreviations (there are ten in all) usually at the end of words, but sometimes in the middle, and the unfamiliar spelling of some words, e.g. '*charissimis*'. The following is a transcription of the part of the note reproduced:

Mitto ad te annotationes meas, ut videas an cum tuis consentiant. Si dabitur oportunitas, cupio scire an hae litterae sint tibi redditae quas misi per quosdam negociatores januenses per quos poteris rescribere.
Opto te cum tibi charissimis, quam prosperrime valere.
Basil. Cal. Junii 1536

Erasmus Rot.
aegra manu

Tho: Moor L. Chancelour

III. THE PORTRAITS OF MORE, WARHAM (Plate VI) AND FISHER (Plate VII) are from sketches made by Holbein between 1526 and 1528. More would be about fifty years of age. He was born in Cheapside in 1478, and as a boy entered the service of Archbishop Morton, Henry VII's Minister, who sent him to Oxford. There he became devoted to the New Learning, and met John Colet and Erasmus. Following his father's profession, he studied Law at Lincoln's Inn, and rose to be an Under-Sheriff of London. In 1518 he entered the royal service, and was successively Under-Treasurer (1521), Speaker of the Commons (1523) and Chancellor (1529) after the fall of Wolsey. He resigned this office in 1532, and in 1535 was tried and executed for denying the Royal Supremacy of the Church.

Reproduced by gracious permission of Her Majesty the Queen.

IV and V. *Above.* A VIEW OF BASEL as Erasmus knew it, from a coloured pen drawing of 1535, by Conrad Morand. It is from the collection which belonged to the son of the printer Boniface Amerbach, a close friend of Erasmus. The building with two spires, seen above the centre of the bridge over the Rhine, is the Cathedral, where Erasmus is buried.

Left. This VENETIAN LONG DAGGER was carried by Erasmus on his journeys. There was considerable danger from robbers, or wandering bands of soldiers, but there is no record of Erasmus having employed this weapon in his defence.

Right, top. AN ENGLISH GOLD COIN, which was in Erasmus' possession. This coin, called a Royal, or Rose Noble from the rose stamped on it, was issued by Edward IV in 1465. Its current value was 10 shillings; when the sovereign of 20s. was issued later, the Royal became the ancestor of our half sovereign.

Right, bottom. A BRONZE MEDAL with a portrait of Erasmus, dated 1519. The Latin inscription says that it is drawn from the life, but a comparison with Holbein's picture shows that the artist has failed with Erasmus' nose, which should be much more pointed.

Right, corner. AN HOUR GLASS which was used by Erasmus. A sculptured relief showing Morpheus holding an hour glass seems to show that it was used in Classical times. Its invention, however, is usually attributed to Luitprand, a monk of Chartres in the 8th century. From the 16th century hour glasses were used in Churches to limit the length of sermons and until recently a 28-second sand glass was used in navigation to determine a ship's rate of knots.

Waramus Arch B' Cant.

VI. WILLIAM WARHAM, Archbishop of Canterbury, the generous patron of Erasmus, was about seventy when Holbein drew him. He was educated at Winchester and New College, and studied Law. He then took Orders, and held several livings, but his activities were mainly diplomatic. He became Bishop of London in 1502, and held the office of Chancellor from 1504 to 1515, being succeeded by Wolsey. In 1505 he became Archbishop of Canterbury, and crowned Henry VIII and Catherine of Aragon in 1509. He played little part in the Royal Divorce proceedings, but in 1531 he protested, though ineffectually, against the 'Submission of the Clergy', and added to Henry's new title of 'Supreme Head of the Church' the words 'as far as the law of Christ allows.' He died in 1532. He was a man of simple and frugal tastes, but a lavish and genial host, fond of a good jest (see Letter 9).

Reproduced by gracious permission of Her Majesty the Queen.

VII. JOHN FISHER, Bishop of Rochester, was about sixty-two when Holbein made this sketch of him, which expresses his simplicity and saintliness. He had a distinguished career at Cambridge and was Chancellor of the University from 1504 until his death. It was through his influence that Erasmus visited Cambridge. Though a supporter of the New Learning, he opposed the Reformation, and was executed in 1535 for refusing to take the Oath of Supremacy.

Reproduced by gracious permission of Her Majesty the Queen.

VIII. JOHANN FROBEN, the printer and publisher of Basel, was painted by Holbein in 1522. The founder of this famous Swiss Press was John Amerbach; Froben joined him as printer, and after his death, worked with Amerbach's three sons. A group of learned men gathered round the establishment, just as they did at Venice round that of Aldus Manutius. One of these was Beatus Rhenanus, to whom Erasmus wrote Letter 18. Erasmus lived in Basel from 1514, and most of his works were published by Froben. Froben's son was Erasmus' godson. The printer was himself a good scholar; Letter 14 is a specimen of his style. This very fine portrait shows a craftsman, determined, energetic and honest.

Reproduced by gracious permission of Her Majesty the Queen.

ERASMUS ROTERODAMUS

It is impossible to be quite certain about all the facts of the early life of Desiderius Erasmus. He was born in Rotterdam on October 27, perhaps in 1466; he was apparently an illegitimate son, and his father was probably a priest. There is some doubt concerning even his name. Some think that he was christened Erasmus after a saint of that name, but the usual view is that his real name was Gerard Gerardson. Gerard means 'Beloved', and Desiderius is bad Latin, and Erasmus bad Greek for 'Beloved'. It is interesting that his godson, the son of his printer, Johann Froben, was christened Erasmius, which is the correct Greek form.

After an unsuccessful attempt to make him a chorister at Utrecht Cathedral, he was sent to a famous school at Deventer, where, by the traditional medieval methods, he acquired a knowledge of Latin, and of very little else. Printing was still in its infancy, and only the teacher would have a book; classes were often enormous (we hear of some containing over two hundred pupils) and the boys sat round copying down laboriously the rules of grammar and syntax, passages from an author, and long traditional comments upon them. The study of Greek was yet to come.

When Erasmus was about fifteen his parents died, and his troubles began. His three guardians had but one idea, to free themselves from their responsibilities as soon as possible by turning the boy into a monk. For a long while Erasmus held out against cajolery and threats; finally his resistance was broken, and he became a monk of the Augustinian Order. He spent eight rather miserable years in the monastery

I

of Steyn, near Gouda; though he had leisure to
study, he found the religious life unsuited both to his
temperament and to his health. At last an opportunity for escape was offered; the Bishop of Cambrai
was looking for a Latin Secretary, and Erasmus, now
an accomplished scholar, was chosen for the post, and
remained in the Bishop's service for about two years.

But this comparative freedom was not enough; his
aim was the pursuit of learning and a University
degree. Finally, in 1495, he induced the Bishop to
send him to Paris to study for the degree of Doctor
of Theology. He entered the College of Montaigu,
but soon found the bad food and living conditions
intolerable to his delicate constitution; in fact, his
chronic ill-health dates from this period. He therefore moved into cheap lodgings, and supplemented
the Bishop's meagre allowance by taking private
pupils. One of his methods of instruction was a
daily interchange of letters in Latin (see Letter 1).
His most distinguished pupil was a young Englishman named William Blount, later Lord Mountjoy.
In 1499 Mountjoy persuaded his tutor to come back
to England with him. Here Erasmus was destined
to meet the two men who became his closest friends,
and had a great effect upon his life and character—
John Colet, afterwards Dean of St Paul's, and Thomas
More, future Lord Chancellor of England.

Mountjoy was already a married man when he
was in Paris, but his wife was only a child, and was
living in Hertfordshire with her father, Sir William
Say. He was intimate with the More family, and
very likely introduced Erasmus to Thomas More, then
a young man of twenty-one. The friendship thus
begun lasted until the death of More on the scaffold
in 1535. Soon after they met, an incident occurred
which caused the rather shy foreign scholar some
embarrassment. On the pretext of a country walk,

More brought Erasmus into a house in Kent, where a group of children were playing. It was Eltham Palace, and the children were the family of King Henry VII. Erasmus soon discovered that some literary composition was expected of him, in honour of the occasion; Prince Henry actually sent him a note demanding it. A poem was duly written, but Erasmus was somewhat annoyed with More for landing him in such a predicament (Letter 4).

But Erasmus enjoyed his stay in England immensely, as we can gather from a somewhat frivolous account of country-house life which he sent to a poet friend of his in Paris, named Faustus Andrelinus. 'The Erasmus you once knew has now become almost a good sportsman, not the worst of riders, and a fairly experienced courtier. You also, if you are wise, will hasten hither'; and he then describes the pleasant English custom of greeting visitors with a kiss. 'There is, too, a custom which cannot be sufficiently praised. Wherever you go, you are welcomed with kisses by everybody; when you depart, you are dismissed with kisses; you come back, and your kisses are returned to you; wherever you turn, everything is full of kisses.' This must not be taken as a serious contribution to a social history of England; Faustus was a flippant and worldly poet, and Erasmus is suiting his style to his correspondent.

But Erasmus was a scholar, not a courtier, and soon found his way to Oxford, where he met John Colet, who was lecturing on the Epistles of St Paul with fervour and originality. Colet urged him to settle down in Oxford as a lecturer, but Erasmus, rather to Colet's annoyance, refused. He had realised, however, from Colet's example, what his life work must be—the restoration of Theology, rescuing it from outworn medieval ideas. To achieve this aim he knew that he must study the New Testament in the

original Greek. He already knew a little Greek, and
in England he met three men who were pioneers in
the language, William Grocyn, Thomas Linacre, and
William Latimer. He decided to go back to his
University in Paris, and gain a thorough knowledge
of the language.

But on his way to the Continent he suffered a
severe blow at the hands of the customs officials at
Dover. He had £20 (at least £300 in modern
valuation) in English currency, and the law forbade
the export of English money. Thomas More, who
as a lawyer should have known better, had assured
him that, since it had not been acquired in England,
the law did not apply to it; but the officials were
adamant, and confiscated all but £2. Money meant
to Erasmus leisure for study, and perhaps a visit to
Italy, the home of learning, and he never ceased to
resent the injury.

Soon after his return to Paris he fell ill with a fever,
and during convalescence compiled a collection of
quotations from the classics, called *Adagia*, to aid
scholars who desired to write elegant Latin. To
show that he bore no grudge against his English
friends over the tragedy at Dover, he dedicated the
book to Lord Mountjoy, and added to it the poem
he had written to celebrate his visit to the royal
children. For years he continued to add to the
Adagia, which ran into sixty editions, and became a
very large collection.

For four years he continued studying in Paris,
except when he fled to Louvain or Orleans to escape
the frequent outbreaks of plague. Then in 1505 we
find him in England again; on this occasion it was
Cambridge, where he received his degree of Bachelor
of Divinity, and London, which at this time contained
almost more men of learning than the Universities.
He usually stayed with More in his new house at the

village of Chelsea; Grocyn and Linacre were by now living in London, and he made the acquaintance of Warham, Archbishop of Canterbury, who became one of his most generous patrons. From several letters we can picture Erasmus travelling by boat with Grocyn up the Thames to Lambeth Palace, to take part in one of those gatherings of scholars in which the learned Archbishop took such delight.

This second visit to England brought Erasmus the long-sought opportunity to visit Italy. In 1506 he set out as tutor to the two sons of Henry VII's physician. He was now a scholar with a European reputation, and his three years' tour was in the nature of a triumphal progress. At Turin he took his Doctor's degree; at Venice he was welcomed by the band of learned men who had gathered round the famous printer Aldus Manutius; here the second edition of the *Adagia* was printed. At Bologna, where he stayed for some time with his two charges, he received from Pope Julius II leave to lay aside his monastic habit. In 1509 he reached Rome, and was welcomed as an equal by the greatest scholars of the day, and strongly urged to remain there. But another invitation, even more attractive, had meanwhile come from England. Henry VII was dead, and the champions of the New Learning hailed with joy the accession of his clever and handsome son. Warham and Mountjoy urged Erasmus to return and take advantage of the favourable situation. He hastened northwards over the Alps, and at the end of the year arrived at Thomas More's house.

Here he wrote within a very short time (he himself says a week) the book for which he is perhaps most famous; at any rate, it is probably the only one of his works that is read nowadays. This is the *Praise of Folly*, or *Encomium Moriae*, as he called it, with a pun on the name of More. He had jotted down notes for the book on his long journey from Italy, and at his first arrival at Chelsea an attack of lumbago confined him to the house, and gave him enforced leisure to write. The book is a satire upon the ignorance, stupidity and superstition of the world. Folly speaks in person, and deals unsparingly with all classes of men, not excepting the Church, but with such refinement of wit that no one could take offence at it. But the book set men thinking, and had considerable influence upon the Reformation.

Erasmus spent five years in England (1509–14), but after the composition of the *Praise of Folly* there is a gap of two years, during which he disappears from view, and no letters of his exist. We hear of him next in Cambridge, where he was sent by John Fisher, Bishop of Rochester, who had been President of Queens' College. His rooms were in a turret of Queens', still called 'Erasmus' Tower.' He gave lectures in Greek, and was elected Lady Margaret Reader in Divinity. He did not earn enough to live on; in fact, sometimes there were no undergraduates to lecture to, because the town was visited by the plague, and the University was entirely deserted. His friends, however, came to his assistance. Lord Mountjoy gave him a small pension, and Warham presented him with the living of Aldington, in Kent. He could not discharge his duties as a parish priest —for one thing, he could not speak enough English— so he was allowed to resign and take two-thirds of the stipend, paying the rest to a curate to do the work for him.

But the high hopes which had brought him to England—he may have had thoughts of being made a Privy Councillor—had by now faded. Henry was involved in a European war, and had lost interest in the New Learning. But before Erasmus left England he had helped Colet in the foundation of his new school of St Paul's, and had written some elementary Latin books for the use of the scholars. His time at Cambridge also had not been wasted; he had written much on the Christian Fathers, and begun his work on the Greek text of the New Testament.

Leaving Cambridge in 1514, he went to Basel, where he spent most of the remaining twenty-two years of his life. For some time he tried to live in Louvain, where he had a house, but the virulent and bigoted opposition of the monks soon drove him away. Religious strife caused him to leave Basel for six years (1529–35), but he returned for the last year of his life. His last two visits to England, in 1516 and 1517, were very short; it was on his return from the second that he endured a perilous landing on the coast near Boulogne, mentioned in Letter 15.

The year 1516 saw the publication of two books which have had considerable influence, More's *Utopia* and Erasmus' Greek text of the New Testament, dedicated to Pope Leo X. The latter, in addition to the Greek text, contained a new Latin version more accurate than the old Vulgate. He added later a series of paraphrases of the New Testament books, giving simple explanations of them for the unlearned reader. In his preface, he expresses his desire that the Scriptures should be translated into all languages, and thus be accessible to all men: 'I long for the ploughboy to sing them as he follows the plough, the weaver to hum them to the tune of his shuttle, the traveller to beguile with them the dullness of his journey.' In the same year he brought out his great edition of the works of St Jerome; his aim was to get behind the medieval interpretations of Christianity to the Fathers of the Early Church.

Erasmus saw clearly the shortcomings of the Church of his day, and his purpose, like that of the other Humanists such as Colet and More, was to reform the Church *from within* by sound learning combined with common sense. In the *Praise of Folly* he had employed the weapon of satire against monkish superstitions. But a year after the publication of the New Testament a friar of Wittenberg, named Martin Luther, nailed to the church door his famous ninety-five arguments against Indulgences, and thus began that violent reformation of the Church *from without*, shattering its age-old institutions, and asserting the right of each individual to approach God through the mediation of Christ alone, instead of through that of the priests; the right of private judgment was set up against obedience to the ancient authority of the Church. All this was clean contrary to the ideals of Erasmus, and bitter feeling arose between him and Luther. He was attacked from both sides; some Catholics called him a heretic, the Lutherans a coward; but he never wavered. To the end of his life he still pursued his aim—reform through knowledge; and he still kept his independence, though the Pope offered to make him a Cardinal the year before his death.

Only a few of his writings have so far been mentioned; the full list would be of formidable length. He edited most of the Christian Fathers, and several Classical authors, such as Terence and Seneca. His most popular work, next to the *Adagia*, was the *Colloquia*, a series of dialogues in which various characters discuss topics of current interest with lively humour. The object of the book was partly educational, to introduce the pupil as quickly as possible to the reading of Latin, without too much insistence upon grammar; partly moral and religious. It was dedicated to his six-year-old godson, Johann Erasmius Froben, the son of his printer at Basel.

Cicero's correspondence is voluminous, but it is nothing to that of Erasmus. He had friends in every country of Europe, and the letters which he wrote and received fill eight bulky volumes in the latest edition. He spent a great part of his life in England, France and Germany, but does not seem to have been able to speak the languages of those countries with any degree of fluency. Fortunately, all educated people spoke and wrote in Latin; it was a real universal language. This was not the debased variety of Latin which was used before the Renaissance; Erasmus' style is marked by a copious vocabulary, and an extraordinary command of the best classical idiom. Apart from some medieval peculiarities of spelling, and occasional lapses in syntax due to haste in writing, there is nothing of which Cicero or Terence would seriously have disapproved. This applies also to most of Erasmus' correspondents whose letters appear in this selection: Cuthbert Tunstall, Bishop of Durham, Warham, Fisher, and Johann Froben the printer. That the Dean of St Paul's should be guilty of failing to use the subjunctive mood in Indirect Questions is perhaps a sidelight on his impetuous and pugnacious character (Letter 11).

Let us take leave of Erasmus by reading part of a letter which he wrote to the Bishop of Cracow in August 1535, a year before his death. He has just returned to Basel from Freiburg; he is in failing health, and clearly does not expect to live long; the recent executions of Sir Thomas More and the Bishop of Rochester have been a heavy blow to him. (The letter is in the abridged form, from Froude's *Life and Letters of Erasmus*.)

'Whatever I write, however carelessly, finds its way into type, and I cannot prevent it. They have even got hold of old exercises of mine at school, and publish them for what they can make by it.

'I was dangerously ill in the spring; I was ordered change of air, and was carried back to Basel in a chair in which for several years I had driven about in Freiburg. The Basel people had prepared a set of rooms which they thought would please me. The city which I left six years back in revolution is now quiet and orderly. I do not mean to stay long; I shall return to Freiburg when a house I have bought there is ready for me. Later, perhaps, I may go into Burgundy, the wine of that country being necessary for my health. The carriers spoil what they bring here by opening the casks and diluting what they leave with water.

'But indeed I cannot hope ever to be well again, either here or anywhere. I was delicate as a child; I had too thin a skin, and suffered from changes of the weather. In my stronger days I did not mind my infirmities, but now that I am but skin and bone I feel them all again. My comfort is that the end cannot be far off.

'You will learn from a letter which I enclose the fate of Sir Thomas More and the Bishop of Rochester. They were the wisest and most saintly men that England had. In the death of More I feel as if I had died myself; we had but one soul between us.

'The Pope has created some new Cardinals, and proposed to make me one of them; they offer me other dignities, which I shall not accept. A poor, half-dead wretch such as I am cannot be tempted into grand, idle company, merely that I may end my life as a rich man. I am pleased by the Pope's letter to me, but the ox is not fit for the saddle.'

In his early life Erasmus was terrified by the thought of death, but when it came he received it with calmness. He died peacefully on July 12, 1536, and was buried in Basel Cathedral.

ERASMUS AND HIS TIMES

1. A Boarding-house in Paris

In 1495, Erasmus' patron, the Bishop of Cambrai, sent him to Paris to study for his degree of Doctor of Theology, making him an allowance which Erasmus considered rather too moderate. He entered the College of Montaigu, but his delicate constitution could not stand the rough and scanty fare, and in 1496 he moved into lodgings, kept by the wife of a minor official of the Court of Charles VIII. He had to eke out the Bishop's allowance by taking pupils, among whom were two young men from Lübeck, Henry and Christian Northoff. One of his methods of teaching them Latin was a daily interchange of letters in that language; the brothers were not actually living with Erasmus. The following piece is part of a letter sent to Christian Northoff in the early part of 1497. It gives us a vivid, if slightly exaggerated, picture of life in a students' lodging-house four hundred and fifty years ago.

ERASMUS CHRISTIANO S.D.

There had been high words between the landlady and the maid, in the course of which the former had resorted to blows. In a conversation afterwards, I advised the girl to pull off her mistress's false hair next time. This was, of course, said in jest. But about supper-time our host, in great trepidation, summoned us to behold a terrible spectacle—mistress and maid engaged in a violent struggle, with hair all over the place. The combatants were only separated with difficulty. At supper the lady complained bitterly of the maid's outrageous conduct. I made some soothing remarks, and

11

congratulated myself that she had no suspicion of the part I
had played in the tragedy.

Spectavimus hodie matremfamilias cum famula
domestica fortiter depugnantem. Sonuerat diu tuba
ante congressum, convicia fortiter utrimque regerun-
tur. Hic aequo Marte discessum est, triumphavit
5 nemo. Haec in hortis, nos e cenaculo taciti specta-
bamus, non sine risu. Sed audi catastrophen.
A pugna conscendit cubiculum meum puella, concinnatura lectos. Inter confabulandum laudo
fortitudinem illius, quod voce conviciisque nihil
10 cesserit dominae; ceterum optasse me ut, quantum
lingua valebat, tantundem valuisset et manibus.
Nam hera, virago robusta ut vel athleta videri posset,
subinde caput humilioris puellae pugnis contundebat.
'Usque adeone' inquam 'nullos habes ungues, ut
15 ista impune feras?' Respondit illa subridens sibi
quidem non tam animum deesse quam vires. 'An
tu putas' inquam 'bellorum exitus a viribus tantum
pendere? Consilium ubique valet plurimum.'
Roganti quid haberem consilii, 'Ubi te rursus
20 adorietur,' inquam, 'protinus caliendrum detrahe'
(nam mulierculae Parisiorum mire sibi placent nigris
quibusdam caliendris): 'eo detracto mox in capillos
invola.'

Haec ut a me ioco dicebantur, itidem accipi
25 putabam. Atqui sub cenae tempus accurrit anhelus
hospes; is erat Caroli regis caduceator, vulgato
cognomine dictus Gentil Gerson. 'Adeste,' inquit,
'domini mei, videbitis cruentum spectaculum.'
Accurrimus, offendimus matremfamilias ac puellam

humi colluctantes. Vix a nobis diremptae sunt. 30
Quam cruenta fuisset pugna res ipsa declarabat.
Iacebant per humum sparsa, hic caliendrum illic
flammeum. Glomeribus pilorum plenum erat solum;
tam crudelis fuerat laniena. Ubi accubuimus in
cena, narrat nobis magno stomacho materfamilias 35
quam fortiter se gessisset puella. 'Ubi pararem' inquit
'illam castigare, hoc est pugnis contundere, illa mihi
protinus caliendrum detraxit e capite.' Agnovi me
non surdae cecinisse fabulam. 'Id detractum' inquit
'mihi venefica vibrabat in oculos.' Id non ad- 40
monueram. 'Tum' inquit 'tantum capillorum evulsit
quantum hic videtis.' Caelum ac terram testata est
se nunquam expertam esse puellam tam pusillam ac
perinde malam. Nos excusare casus humanos et
ancipitem bellorum exitum, tractare de componenda 45
in posterum concordia. Ego interim mihi gratulabar
dominae non subolere rem meo consilio gestam;
alioqui sensissem et ipse illi non deesse linguam.

2. TUTOR TO PARENT

Henry Northoff—the Henricus of this letter—had
introduced to Erasmus another pupil from Lübeck.
We do not know his name, but he seems to have been
more bother than he was worth, and his father appears
to have been slack in paying his bills. He was partly
in the care of a scholar named Augustine Vincent,
as were also the Northoff brothers. This letter
(December 1498) from Erasmus to the boy's father is
a model of tact; the situation is one which might
sometime confront the modern housemaster.

ERASMUS CUIDAM LUBECENSI S.D.

1–34. *I have been tutoring your son for some months, and he is now living in my house. I have supplied him with everything he needed, and have done my best to make him worthy of his teacher and his father. He is an able and reasonably docile pupil.*

I am surprised, however, that his books have not yet come, and that I have not received the fees agreed upon. Augustine, who looked after him while I was away for reasons of health, has received a small sum, which I had to supplement from my own pocket. There is a good deal of fever about in Paris, and, since health is so important, I should like to know whether you would agree to my taking him further away from the city.

Salve, vir integerrime. Filius tuus apud me vivit et a me docetur, iis quidem condicionibus quas ab Henrico accepi, qui mihi nomine tuo triginta duos coronatos et vestem promisit. Aegrotavit graviter
5 nuper, sed convaluit Dei beneficio et medicorum opera. Fuit in tutela mea complusculos menses, quibus ei quibus opus erat suppeditavi. Mense Octobri puerum in familiam meam adiunxi; curatur a me non ut alienus, sed ut ex me natus. Ingenio
10 praeditus est singulari; mores pro ea aetate tractabiles sunt et tolerabiles. Dabo operam, quantum quidem in me erit, ut tibi eum restituam et me praeceptore et te patre dignum. Libros eius nondum ad manus meas perferri miror. Antuuerpiensis ille mercator
15 scripsit se per quendam mercatorem Parisiensem transmisisse, et eum nominat; verum is constanter negat. Pecunias adhuc nullas eius nomine accepi.

Augustinus, sub cuius tutela erat, dum ego valetudinis causa in patria abessem, ab Henrico quinque aut sex florenos sese accepisse fatetur. Is eum tres menses 20 et aluit et docuit, quod ego me tum in Italiam concessurum putabam. Ei eas pecunias reliqui pro opera sua; praeterea quod de ratione diminutum erat adieci, apud illum enim aegrotabat: praeterea meo sumptu vestitus est. Coeperat hic nescioquae 25 febris pullulascere, sed non admodum frequens; quare in locum urbis apertissimum atque saluber- rimum demigravi. Quod malum si repullulaverit, longius forte concedam. Nihil enim nobis salute antiquius esse debet et vita. Nam bene vivere, nisi 30 vivamus, non possumus. Qua in re de tua sententia certior fieri cupio, placeatne puerum me consequi. Narrabat enim Henricus, etiamsi filium tuum in Italiam duxissem, me id te approbante facturum.

35–55. *Now what are your wishes for the boy's future? (By the way, do not send money or letters to Paris, but to the merchant of Antwerp, in case they go astray in my absence.) What profession do you intend for him, and what line of study should he pursue? It is most important to have an aim in life. This is rather a long letter, and I have written in Latin, because you might not understand my Dutch. Accept my best wishes for yourself and your family, and assure yourself that I shall do my best for your son.*

Habes de rebus nostris omnibus; reliquum est ut 35 de toto animo tuo nos facias certiores; verum neque pecunias neque literas, nisi per certissimum tabel- larium, miseris, nec Parisios miseris, sed ad eum mercatorem Antuuerpiensem, ne, si hinc concessero,

40 illae ad alienas manus perferantur. Hoc quoque ad
me perscribas velim, cui vitae generi filium tuum
destinaris, et quibus potissimum literis imbui placeat.
Finis enim unaquaque in re praefigi debet, ad quem
omnia tamquam ad signum conferantur. Nam
45 quanquam omni quidem literarum genere pueri sint
instituendi, refert tamen quo sua studia destinent, ut
cum omnia perdiscere non liceat saltem aptissima
discamus.

Haec pluribus ad te scripsi quam debui, et quidem
50 Latine, non fastidio linguae nostratis, sed quod neque
facile id potuissem, neque tu facile intellexisses. Te
cum optima coniuge tua universaque familia bene
valere precor. De me ita tibi tuisque persuadeas, in
instituendo filio mihi neque fidem neque sollicitu-
55 dinem neque diligentiam defuturam. Lutetiae.

3. A Fit of Depression

Poverty and ill-health dogged Erasmus' footsteps
for a large part of his life, but they never crushed
his indomitable spirit. Like many geniuses, he was
extremely careless with money, and had to stoop to
writing countless begging letters in pursuit of it. Even
when he was receiving adequate pensions from various
patrons we find him complaining of straitened circumstances. He never enjoyed robust health, and was
always terrified of illness, running away from Paris to
Orleans or Louvain whenever epidemics threatened.
It is surprising that he managed to live to the age of
seventy.

During his years in Paris, his great longing was to

visit Italy, and take a degree there. It was not until 1506 that the opportunity came. He travelled with the two young sons of Henry VII's physician, Dr Baptista, and visited among other cities Bologna, where he took his degree, Venice, and Rome. It was at Venice that an edition of his *Adagia* was produced by the famous printer Aldus. (For the *Adagia*, see letters 5 and 6.)

Little is known of the man to whom this letter was written, Arnold Bostius, except that he was a Carmelite friar of Ghent, and a friend of most of the literary men of his day.

ERASMUS ARNOLDO

I am slowly recovering from a prolonged fever; I have lost all ambition, and my only desire is for a peaceful and studious existence. I am a tender plant, and University life is too rigorous for me.

I had hoped to visit Italy this year and take my degree, but the journey is too long and costly. The Bishop of Cambrai is not over-generous; he promises more than he performs. Perhaps it is my fault for not pressing him hard enough.

Salve, mi Arnolde. Iam sesquimensem graviter laboro febri nocturna, lenta quidem illa sed quotidiana, quae me penitus exstinxit. Nondum sum morbo liber, sed tamen aliquanto recreatior; nondum vivo, sed affulget aliqua vitae spes. Petis ut tibi animi mei 5 consilium communicem; hoc unum habe, mundum mihi iamdudum obolere; damno spes meas. Nihil aliud cupio quam mihi dari otium, in quo possim totus uni Deo vivere, deflere peccata aetatis inconsultae, versari in scripturis sacris, aliquid aut 10 legere aut scribere. Id in secessu aut collegio non possum. Nihil enim me tenerius; nec vigilias, nec

2

ieiunia, nec ulla incommoda fert haec valetudo, etiam
cum est prosperrima.   Hic ubi tantis in deliciis vivo,
15 subinde in morbum incido; quid facerem inter
labores collegiales?

Decreveram in Italiam hoc anno concedere, et
Bononiae aliquot menses theologiae operam dare,
atque illic doctoris insigne accipere, deinde in anno
20 iubileo Romam visere; quibus confectis ad meos redire
atque istic vitam componere.   Sed vereor ne haec ut
volumus conficere non possimus.   Metuo imprimis
ne tantum iter et regionis aestum valetudo haec non
ferat.   Denique reputo nec in Italiam veniri nec illic
25 vivi sine summo sumptu. Ad titulum quoque
parandum grandi summa est opus.   Et Episcopus
Cameracensis dat perparce.   Omnino benignius amat
quam largitur, et prolixius omnia pollicetur quam
praestat.   Ipse propemodum in causa sum qui non
30 instem; et sunt tam multi qui vel extorqueant.
Faciam tamen pro tempore quod factu videbitur
optimum.   Bene vale.

4. A Visit to the Court of Henry VII

Erasmus' most important pupil in Paris was the young
Englishman, William Blount, who later succeeded his
father as Lord Mountjoy.   In the summer of 1499
Erasmus was brought over to England by him, and,
while staying near Greenwich, was visited by Thomas
More, whose acquaintance he had made in London.
In the course of a country walk they came to Eltham
Palace, and paid their respects to the royal children,
who were living there with their tutor, the poet John

Skelton. The following narrative comes, not from a letter, but from a *Catalogue* of his writings which Erasmus wrote in 1523; in it he explains the circumstances under which his various compositions came to be written. Piece 5 is from the same source.

This is the story of how I came to write a poem in praise of Henry VII and England—a long task, since I was out of practice. Thomas More took me for a country walk, and landed me in a royal palace, in the midst of Henry's children, the young Henry, Margaret, Mary and Edmund. More presented Henry with some complimentary composition, but I had nothing ready, of course. I was a bit annoyed with More for not having warned me, but I promised the Prince that I would produce something. I went home, and finished the poem in three days.

Edidimus olim carmen de laudibus regis Henrici septimi et illius liberorum, nec non ipsius Britanniae. Is erat labor tridui, et tamen labor, quod iam annos aliquot nec legeram nec scripseram ullum carmen. Id partim pudor a nobis extorsit, partim dolor. 5 Pertraxerat me Thomas Morus, qui tum me in praedio Montioii agentem inviserat, ut animi causa in proximum vicum exspatiaremur. Nam illic educabantur omnes liberi regii, uno Arturo excepto, qui tum erat natu maximus. Ubi ventum erat in 10 aulam, convenit tota pompa, non solum domus illius verum etiam Montioiicae. Stabat in medio Henricus annos natus novem, iam tum indolem quandam regiam prae se ferens, hoc est animi celsitudinem cum singulari quadam humanitate coniunctam. A 15 dextris erat Margareta, undecim ferme annos nata, quae post nupsit Jacobo Scotorum regi. A sinistris

Maria lusitans annos nata quattuor.   Nam Edmondus
adhuc infans in ulnis gestabatur.   Morus cum Arnoldo
20 sodali salutato puero Henrico, quo rege nunc
floret Britannia, nescioquid scriptorum obtulit.   Ego,
quoniam nihil huiusmodi exspectabam, nihil habens
quod exhiberem, pollicitus sum aliquo pacto meum
erga   ipsum   studium   aliquando   declaraturum.
25 Interim subirascebar Moro quod non praemonuisset,
et eo magis quod puer, epistolio inter prandendum
ad me misso, meum calamum provocaret.   Abii
domum, ac vel invitis Musis, cum quibus iam longum
fuerat divortium, carmen intra triduum absolvi.

5. RETURNING GOOD FOR EVIL

This extract from the *Catalogue* explains how
Erasmus' most popular book, the *Adagia*, came to be
written.   On 27 January, 1500, he was about to make
the Channel crossing from Dover to Boulogne.   He
had £20 in his pocket, and had been assured by
Thomas More and Lord Mountjoy that he would
have no trouble at the Customs, because his money
had been changed into French currency.   But they
had mistaken the law, for a statute of Edward III,
re-enacted by Henry VII, forbade the exportation of
gold and silver; property transported abroad must
go in the shape of English goods, to encourage English
industries.   In consequence, all but £2 was taken
from Erasmus, a calamity which he never forgot.   But
it may have saved his life for all that, because on
the journey to Paris he fell into the clutches of a set
of crooks at Amiens, who plotted to rob him with
violence, supposing him to be well supplied with cash.

It was only when they found out their mistake that they allowed him to proceed on his way unharmed.

For the moment, however, Erasmus was very bitter about his misadventure at Dover, and his English friends feared that he would avenge himself by writing something violent about England, or even about Henry VII, which would make another visit to the country impossible. But Erasmus was too wise and fair-minded to take this course; and, to show that his mind was not occupied with his private misfortunes, he wrote and published a book he called the *Adagia*, a collection of popular sayings, quotations, anecdotes, and epigrams, designed to be useful to those who wished to write elegant and classical Latin. During the rest of his life he brought out edition after edition of this 'best seller', until the book was many times the size of the original draft written in 1500. No one reads the book now, but an age which possessed no efficient dictionaries, and considered a sound Latin style important, welcomed it with enthusiasm. Archbishop Warham, for instance, carried his copy about with him wherever he went.

At Dover I lost all my scanty store of money. More and Mountjoy had assured me that there was no danger, since I had no English currency, and the money I possessed had not been acquired in England. But the law forbade the export of any money in excess of six 'angels'.

I expect everyone thought that I would avenge myself upon England by writing something uncomplimentary about her. I was also afraid that Mountjoy might imagine that my feelings towards him were changed. In order to clear myself of any such suspicions, I hastily compiled a collection of Latin quotations, which I dedicated to Mountjoy, adding to it the poem I have just mentioned.

In litore Douariensi, priusquam ingrederer mare,
naufragium fecit tota mea pecunia, quae tum erat
exigua, sed tamen mihi maxima, cum nihil superesset.
Id factum est a praefecto, paene dixeram a praedone,
5 litoris regio nomine, cum mihi Morus ac Montioius
persuasissent nihil esse periculi, nisi monetam Britannicam efferrem. At ego nec Britannicam habebam
nec in Anglia partam aut acceptam. Verum in
litore didici non esse fas ullam efferre pecuniam, ne
10 ferream quidem, ultra pretium sex angelatorum.
Tanti mihi constitit unicam legem Britannicam
didicisse. Ubi nudus rediissem Lutetiam, non dubi-
tabam quin multi exspectarent futurum ut, quod
solent literati, fortunam hanc ulciscerer calamo,
15 scribens aliquid in odium regis aut Angliae; simulque
verebar ne Guilhelmus Montioius, quoniam dederat
occasionem perdendae pecuniae, subvereretur ne
verterem animum erga se meum. Ut igitur et
illorum exspectationem fallerem, immo potius ut
20 declararem me non esse tam iniquum ut privatum
casum imputarem regioni, aut tam incogitantem ut
ob iacturam tantulam vel in me vel in amicos quos
in Anglia reliqueram provocarem tanti principis
iram, simulque Montioio testatum facerem me nihilo
25 secius affectum esse in amicitia quam antea fueram
affectus, visum est protinus aliquid edere. Cum
nihil esset ad manum, tumultuarie paucorum dierum
lectione congessi silvam aliquam Adagiorum, divinans
hoc libelli, qualisqualis esset, vel ob utilitatem
30 versaturum in manibus studiosorum. Hoc argumento
declaravi quam non refrixissem in amicitia. Tum

adiecto carmine, cuius ante memini, testificatus sum
quam non essem offensus vel regi vel regioni ob
pecuniam ereptam. Ea moderatio candorque mihi
tum plurimos amicos conciliavit apud Britannos, 35
viros eruditos, probos ac potentes.

6. AN APPRECIATION OF THE *Adagia*

Faustus Andrelinus was an Italian poet who spent
most of his life in France. He was a brilliant and
popular lecturer in the University of Paris, and in
1496 was appointed Poet Laureate by Charles VIII.
He was one of Erasmus' first friends in Paris, and the
friendship was a lasting one, in spite of the great
difference in their characters. The following letter
which he wrote to Erasmus in June 1500, just when
the *Adagia* was being printed, was incorporated in the
book, together with a letter of dedication to Lord
Mountjoy.

FAUSTUS ANDRELINUS POETA REGIUS HERASMO SUO S.

I am delighted with your Adagia. *The book is
both pleasant and useful, and I strongly urge you to publish
it. You need not be afraid of adverse criticism.*

Legi ego non sine maxima voluptate quae ad me
misisti Adagia, dulcissime Herasme. Ea sunt mea
quidem sententia quae vel inimico iudice probari
possint; adeo utile dulci commiscent, ut omnia certe
suffragantium puncta promereantur. Tam iucundas 5
tamque frugiferas lucubrationes ut in publicum
proferas non hortor modo, verum etiam familiari

quodam iure praecipio, ne scilicet videaris omnino
vel sudorem tuum vel exspectatam iamdiu editionem
10 aspernari. Neque timendi sunt hi qui aliena scripta
subsannare soleant. Non debent nasutum quempiam
rhinocerota formidare, cum non parvam sint et
oblectationem et utilitatem allatura.

Parisii, MCCCCC, xv Iunii.

7. The Founding of St Paul's School

In 1521, a German friend of Erasmus asked him
for a sketch of the life of John Colet, Dean of St Paul's,
and he sent him a very full description of Colet's
career and character. The following piece, describing
the foundation of St Paul's School in 1510–11, is an
extract from this letter. Erasmus was at that time
making his third visit to England. As Froude
puts it in his *Life and Letters of Erasmus*, 'he had
two friends in England between whom and himself
there grew up a more than affectionate intimacy.
With Dean Colet he travelled about the country,
helped him to found St Paul's School, went on
pilgrimages, went to the shrine of Our Lady of
Walsingham, visited Becket's tomb at Canterbury,
saw the saint's dirty shoes which were offered to the
pious to kiss, and gathered the materials for the
excellent pictures of England and English life which
are scattered through his Colloquies. With Thomas
More, who was soon to be knighted, he resided when
in London, at the new house which More had built
at Chelsea.'

*Colet used the wealth inherited from his father in
building a fine school in St Paul's Churchyard, with a house*

for the two schoolmasters. The school is divided into four parts, one of which is used as a chapel. Each boy has his own seat, and the classes are limited to sixteen. There is an entrance examination.

Quicquid e sacerdotiis redibat, id in usus domesticos oeconomo suo dispensandum reliquit; quod erat patrimonii (erat autem amplissimum) ipse in pios usus distribuebat. Nam patre defuncto, cum ingentem pecuniae vim accepisset ex hereditate, ne 5 servata gigneret in eo aliquid morbi, novam scholam exstruxit in coemeterio Sancti Pauli, puero Iesu sacram, opere magnifico. Adiecit aedes magnificas, in quibus agerent duo ludi magistri, quibus amplum salarium designavit, quo gratuito docerent, sed sic 10 uti schola non capiat nisi certum numerum. Eam distinxit in partes quattuor. Primus ingressus habet ceu catechumenos. Nullus autem admittitur nisi qui iam norit et legere et scribere. Secunda pars habet eos quos hypodidascalus instituit. Tertia quos 15 superior erudit. Alteram ab altera dirimit velum quoddam, quod adducitur ac diducitur cum libet. Supra cathedram praeceptoris sedet puer Iesus singulari opere, docentis gestu, quem totus grex adiens scholam ae relinquens hymno salutat. Et imminet 20 Patris facies dicentis 'Ipsum audite': nam haec verba me auctore ascripsit. In postremo sacellum est, in quo licet rem divinam facere. Tota schola nullos habet angulos aut secessus, adeo ut nec cenaculum sit ullum aut cubiculum. Pueris singulis 25 suus est locus in gradibus paulatim ascendentibus,

distinctis spatiis. Quaeque classis habet sedecim, et
qui in sua classe praecellit, sellulam habet ceteris
paulo eminentiorem. Nec quosvis admittunt temere,
30 sed delectus fit indolis et ingeniorum.

8. A LETTER FROM JOHN COLET

This letter is dated March 1512. It is interesting
as showing Colet's sturdy independence, and his
dislike of bishops. He called them 'wolves, not
shepherds', and had as poor an opinion of them as
he had of monasteries, and the medieval methods of
education. It is significant that in choosing a 'Board
of Governors' for his new school, he selected neither
bishops nor priests, but married laymen of honest
repute; he said he found less corruption in them.
Erasmus tells a story to illustrate Colet's antipathy to
bishops. His own Bishop, the aged FitzJames, complained to the Archbishop that Colet had objected to
the worship of images, and had preached against the
dull English habit of reading sermons; this last point
touched the Bishop closely, as he always read his.
The Archbishop of Canterbury took Colet's side, and
the Bishop had to try a fresh line of attack. Colet
was accused before the King of having preached
against the French War, which was impending. He
certainly hated war, and declared that 'an unjust
peace was preferable to a just war'. But after a long
talk in private Henry was satisfied with the Dean's
loyalty and, calling for a cup of wine, pledged him
with the words 'Let every man choose his own
teacher. Hic est Doctor meus.' After that no one
dared to attack Colet.

*I have heard nothing about you since you went away.
I have been staying with my mother, to comfort her after the
death of my servant, of whom she was very fond. I hear that
one of the bishops has been attacking our new school, calling
it, among other things, 'a home of idolatry'. It just makes
me laugh.*

Profecto, Erasme carissime, de te nihil accepi novi
post tuum hinc discessum. Quodsi postea quippiam
intellexero, faciam (quod iubes) te certiorem. Eram
his diebus ruri apud meam genetricem, ut consolarer
dolentem de morte servi mei, qui interiit in domo 5
illius; quem dilexit loco filii, et flevit mortem illius
plusquam mortem filii sui. Ea nocte qua revertebar
ad urbem, accepi epistolam tuam. Unum tibi
significo ridiculum, quendam episcopum (ut accep-
eram) et eum qui habetur ex sapientioribus, in 10
magno hominum conventu nostram scholam blas-
phemasse, dixisseque me erexisse rem inutilem, immo
malam, immo etiam (ut illius verbis utar) domum
idolatriae. Quod quidem arbitror eum dixisse
propterea quod illic docentur poetae. Ad ista, 15
Erasme, non irascor, sed rideo valde.

9. A Letter from Archbishop Warham

Erasmus' third visit to England resulted from a
pressing invitation from the young King Henry VIII.
Erasmus hoped for great things, aiming perhaps at
a seat on the Privy Council, but Henry was soon
preoccupied with a French war; his patron, Lord

Mountjoy, had to be with his King, war was a costly
business for a noble, and the pension which he had
promised could not yet be paid. Erasmus went to
Cambridge for a time, at the suggestion of the Bishop
of Rochester, who was Chancellor of the University.
He did not enjoy his stay; the plague had spread
there, driving most of the undergraduates away; very
few attended his lectures, he was as usual short of
money, and the cost of living was high. In January
1514 he fell ill with an attack of the 'stone' caused,
as he declared, by the poor quality of the Cambridge
ale. He wrote and told the Archbishop of Canterbury
his troubles, hoping for a present of money from his
Maecenas. Warham's reply (accompanied by a gift)
might well surprise anyone who studies his portrait,
but Erasmus bears witness to his fondness for a good
jest. 'He bubbled over with a very pleasing wit, but
it was never malicious or silly, and he took delight in
the rather broad jokes of his friends.'

GUILHELMUS ARCHIEPISCOPUS CANTUARIENSIS
CANCELLARIUS REGNI ET TOTIUS ANGLIAE
PRIMAS ERASMO ROTERODAMO S.D.

*I hope you are better; you ought to be, since we
have just celebrated the Feast of the Purification. But what
have you to do with 'stones'? You don't want them for
building purposes, as I do. I advise you to get rid of them,
and to assist you to do so, I have given ten 'nobles' to a
London goldsmith for you; I only wish they were ten legions of
'angels'. Gold is a powerful medicine; use it to recover your
health, which you need in order to complete your literary
labours.*

Erasme, si valentibus dicimus salutem in capite
literarum, multo magis convenit aegrotanti tibi optare
salutem; tametsi fausto omine auguror te iampridem

calculis purgatum, saltem posteaquam celebravimus
memoriam purgationis Mariae. Quid sibi volunt 5
saxa in corpusculo tuo? Aut quid super hanc petram
inaedificandum est? Non enim construendo es
magnificas domos vel eiusmodi quippiam, ut opinor.
Quocirca cum non sint e re tua calculi, cures quamprimum te superfluo onere liberare, desque pecuniam 10
ut auferantur hi lapides; secus quam ego quotidie
do pecuniam, ut lapides afferantur ad mea aedificia.
Quod ut facilius facias nec tibi desis, dedi filio
cuiusdam aurifabri Londiniensis decem nobiles, quos
in decem legiones mutatos velim. Id auri pharma- 15
cum nonnihil energiae in se continet; eo utere ad
salutem, quam tibi emere multo pluris cupiam.
Restant enim multa egregia opera per te edenda,
quae nisi valeas obire non queas. Cura ut valeas,
nec nos defraudes aegritudine tua pulcherrima spe et 20
dulcissimo fructu doctrinae tuae.

Ex Londino quinto Feb.

10. LUMBAGO?

Erasmus left England in July 1514, and travelled to
Basel by way of St Omer, Ghent, Louvain, Liége,
and Strasburg; then along the left bank of the Rhine.
(Compare the reverse journey described in Letter 18.)

A note in the margin of one of the manuscripts of
this letter reads, '*spinam dorsi fregit Erasmus*', and he
himself describes his affliction as something 'out of the
common'; those, however, who have suffered from
lumbago will clearly recognise all the symptoms of
that painful malady. We know, too, that Erasmus

was subject to lumbago, because in a letter written
the following year he says that an attack, which
confined him to the house while he was staying with
Sir Thomas More in 1510, gave him leisure to write
one of his most famous books, the *Praise of Folly*.

Letter 10 was written at Ghent, but not sent off
until after his arrival at Basel.

ERASMUS ROTERODAMUS GUILHELMO MONTIOIO

*The Abbot was generous to me, and I parted from
him in a very cheerful frame of mind, but misfortune was
awaiting me. Half-way between Rousselaer and Ghent
my horse shied, and wrenched my spine. The pain was
excruciating; my servant helped me to dismount. Standing
was the least painful position, and I thought I should have
to finish my journey on foot, though Ghent was six miles
away. Finally I managed to mount my horse, and rode
slowly and painfully to Ghent. I could neither stand, nor
sit, nor lie down without agony. I sent for the doctor, and
felt ready to die. Next morning I was much better. I
stayed some days at Ghent, and am now on my way to
Antwerp. I will let you know about my state of health.*

Salve, Maecenas optime. Biduum apud Abbatem
commoratus sum; eos dies multa cum hilaritate
transegimus. Dimisit non sine xenio, pollicitus item
amantissime multa. Denique laeta omnia, et ecce
5 subito me fortuna perdidit docuitque nulli rerum
successui fidendum esse. Vix egressus sum diversorium quoddam, quod est medio ferme spatio inter
Rusellam et Gandavum, cum equus meus visis pannis
aliquot humi stratis consternatur, dumque inflexus
10 paro nescioquid dicere ministro, rursum territus
equus in diversum fertur, atque ita distorquet imam

dorsi spinam ut repente magnis clamoribus cruciatum
intolerabilem testari cogerer. Conor ex equo des-
cendere, non possum; minister manibus exceptum
deponit; saevit dolor nullis explicandus verbis, 15
maxime si corpus inflexissem. Erectus minus afflige-
bar, sed tamen ipse me non poteram erigere semel
incurvatus. Eram illic in agris, nulla diversoria nisi
frigidissima et rusticissima, et aberam a Gandavo sex
maximis passuum milibus. Sensi ambulatione minus 20
saevire malum, et tamen longius erat iter quam ut
vel a sano pedibus confici posset.

Cogita quid mihi hic fuerit animi. Vovi divo
Paulo me commentarios in epistolam ad Romanos
absoluturum, si contingeret hoc periculi evadere. 25
Aliquanto post cum desperarem, coactus sum experiri
num equum possem conscendere; conscendi praeter
spem. Ambulo lente, fero; iubeo ministrum progredi
paulo celerius, fero, tametsi non sine cruciatu.
Gandavum pervenio, descendo ex equo, ingredior 30
cubiculum; ibi dolor se totum prodit, maxime a
quiete. Stare non poteram, nisi a duobus utrimque
sublatus in altum, idque valide; quod si vel paulum
me remisissem, intolerabilis redibat dolor. Nec
sedere poteram, iacens nec tantulum me poteram 35
movere. Accerso medicum et pharmacopolam. Ita
modis omnibus affectus fui ut nihil nisi de morte
cogitarem.

Mane paulum conor me movere lecto; procedit,
sto, moveo, sedeo, nullo sustinente. Ago gratias 40
Deo et Paulo. Manet adhuc sensus mali, maxime
si corpus distorqueam. Itaque Gandavi dies aliquot

commoratus sum, amicis retinentibus et malo ita
suadente: de quo nondum securus sum. Neque
15 enim vulgare fuit, quicquid fuit. Nunc Antuuerpiam
pergam, si modo per morbum licebit; et ubicumque
locorum ero, reddam te de valetudine mea certiorem.
Bene vale.

11. ANOTHER LETTER FROM JOHN COLET

Erasmus sent a letter to Colet on the same day as
the previous one to Lord Mountjoy. His ill-health
was a subject of great interest to himself, and he never
missed a chance of telling his friends about it. He
would frequently write to half a dozen or so, describing
his latest afflictions in some detail, and frequently in
almost the same words. Letter 20 is a good example.
Colet's brief reply was probably written in some haste;
this is the most charitable explanation of his failure to
use the subjunctive mood in Indirect Questions. The
Latin of Erasmus himself is not free from similar
blemishes, due to the same cause.

IOANNES COLETUS DOMINO ERASMO S.

*I am glad to know where you are, and that you
are well. I hope we shall see you again some time. Your
friends here are all well; Warham is his usual kindly self,
Wolsey is now lording it at York, my own Bishop continues
to annoy me. I have thoughts of retiring to a Carthusian
monastery.*

Erasme carissime, accepi literas tuas Basileae
scriptas III Kal. Sept. Gaudeo quod intelligimus

ubinam locorum es et sub quo caelo vivis; gaudeo
etiam quod vales. Fac votum persolvas Paulo, ut
inquis, factum. Maguntiae tanti te factum fuisse 5
quantum scribis, facile credo. Gaudeo te reversurum
aliquando ad nos; tamen non possum id sperare. Tui
hic omnes valent; Cantuariensis semper est solita
suavitate, Lincolniensis regnat nunc Eboracensis,
Londiniensis non cessat vexare me. Cotidie meditor 10
meum secessum et latibulum apud Cartusienses.
Nidus noster prope perfectus est. Reversus ad nos,
quantum conicere possum, illic mortuum mundo
me reperies. Tu cura ut valeas, et quo te conferes
fac sciam. 15

Vale ex Londino xx^{mo} die Octobr.

12. Asking for an Introduction

Willibald Pirckheimer was a learned and wealthy
citizen of Nuremberg, of which city he became a
Councillor. He was later made an Imperial Councillor by the Emperor Maximilian. On his retirement
he devoted his time to literary pursuits, and to the
education of his five daughters, who became famous
for their learning. He was a generous patron of art
and literature; the artist Dürer illustrated some of
his works.

This letter to a great friend of Erasmus, Beat Bild
of Rheinau, shows the high position which Erasmus
had attained among the literary men of Europe. He
urges Beat to secure for him an introduction to
Erasmus; the appeal was successful, and the two
became friends, and corresponded frequently.

BILIBALDUS PIRCKHEYMERIUS BEATO RHENANO S.D.

*Our friendship was due, you will remember, to the
kind offices of Peutunger. Will you perform a similar service
for me? I hear that Erasmus is in Basel, and am desirous
of making his acquaintance. Though I enjoy the favour of
a host of distinguished and learned men, yet I should value
most of all the friendship of so great a scholar. I should be
greatly indebted to you if you would use your best efforts to
secure this. If only you could bring Erasmus with you when
you come to see me!*

Meministi, ut arbitror, vir optime, intercessione
Conradi Peutunger, amici communis, amicitiae iure
te mihi conciliatum esse. Eandem operam nunc
quoque a te familiariter vicissim exigo; audio
5 siquidem Erasmum Roterodamum, non absque
honoris praefatione nominandum, Basileae nunc
agere; quem unum ex omnibus incognitis notissimum
mihi amicitia copulari summopere cuperem. Quamvis enim gratiam Imperialem meruerim, variorum
10 principum favorem acquisiverim, hominum clarorum
ac doctorum familiaritatem consecutus sim, reliqua
denique amicorum turba belle mihi pollere videar,
amicitiam tamen viri tam eruditi ac clari non in
ultimis bonis collocarem, sed et rebus pretiosissimis
15 longe anteponerem. Tu itaque enitere, oro, ut
amicitiam tanti viri acquirere valeam, qua re nihil
mihi gratius facere poteris. Promisisti te aliquando
(in literis) huc venturum; o si talem mihi adduceres
hospitem, qua benevolentia, quanto illum prosequerer
20 amore! Spero enim ac animus spondet, me ex

humanis non excessurum priusquam illum viderim coramque alloqui detur. Amici igitur tu satisfacias desiderio, quem nullo maiore officio demereri poteris. Vale.

Ex Nuremberga nona Decembris. 25

13. A LETTER TO THOMAS LINACRE

Thomas Linacre (1460–1520) was a pioneer in the study of Greek. He was educated in the Monastery School of Christ Church, Canterbury, under the famous Prior Selling, himself one of the earliest Greek scholars in England. He went to Italy in the suite of Prior Selling, who was Henry VII's ambassador to the Pope, and spent about five years there, studying Greek and Medicine. Returning to Oxford, he was one of Erasmus' Greek teachers in 1497. From about 1500 he lived in London and devoted himself to medicine, becoming one of the King's Physicians in 1509. His patients included Cardinal Wolsey, Archbishop Warham and Erasmus. He is best remembered as one of the founders of the Royal College of Physicians in 1518; the College was given the sole right of licensing physicians in London.

ERASMUS ROTERODAMUS THOMAE LINACRO MEDICO
REGIO S.D.

My New Testament has won favour with men of learning, and even with theologians. A sudden fever has prevented me from sailing, on medical advice. Would you please send me a copy of the prescription I used in London; my servant left it at the apothecary's.

Tametsi novum non erat, tamen gratissimum fuit quod ex Mori literis cognovi te tam amice nobis favere, licet immerentibus. Novum Testamentum adeo placet ubique doctis, etiam ex ordine theo-
5 logorum, ut indocti pudore obticescant. Febricula subito oborta fuit in causa quominus me navigationi commiserim, praesertim dissuadente medico Ghisberto. Maiorem in modum te rogo ut pharmacum, quod, cum essem proxime Londini, sumpsi te
10 auctore, denuo descriptum mihi transmittas; nam puer schedulam apud pharmacopolam reliquit. Erit id mihi gratissimum. Cetera ex Moro cognosces. Bene vale.

Ex divo Audumaro.   Nonis Juliis.

14. PRINTER TO AUTHOR

A letter dated June 17, 1516, from John Froben, the printer of Basel, who printed the great majority of Erasmus' books. He worked with the three sons of his late partner, John Amerbach, and the publishing side of the business was managed by a bookseller named Lachner, whose daughter Gertrude was Froben's second wife. Her son, Erasmius Froben, was Erasmus' godson. Erasmus lived for many years in Basel, chiefly between 1514 and 1516 and between 1521 and 1529. Religious troubles caused him to migrate to Freiburg in 1529, but he returned in 1535, and died there the following year.

I am sending you some manuscripts which arrived after you had left. Your book De Principis Institutione *is now printed, and the* Jerome *is nearly ready. I have been*

*held up for paper, but shall get some from Strasburg, if the
price is satisfactory. The Freiburg copy of* Jerome *is
defective, and I cannot print it, to my disappointment. I
shall take great care over the printing of the* Moria. *We
look forward to your return, and all send our good wishes.*

S.D. Quas a te literas proximis post discessum
tuum diebus accepimus, Breve videlicet Leonis Pont.,
commendationis ad Britanniae Regem exemplum,
cum aliis adiunctis, et Reuchlini Picheymerique
Norinbergensis epistolas nunc misimus. Libellus tuus 5
de Principis Institutione una cum aliis quibusdam in
officina nostra absolutus est. Hieronymus ad finem
tendit. Laboravimus aliquamdiu chartaria inopia,
quod Lotharingiae ad nos clausus esset aditus; id
quod tu non sine damno fuisti expertus. Sed haec 10
res nos non impediet. Nam Argentina sat chartarum
nobis suppeditabit, si modo pretium, quod paulo
maius est, arriserit. Commentarium sub Hieronymi
titulo quod Fryburgi describebatur omittere cogimur:
mutilum enim est; nam desunt tum in medio tum 15
in calce nonnullae pagellae. Excidimus igitur a spe
nostra qua sperabamus nos quiddam novi prolaturos
quod hactenus paucissimis fuisset cognitum. Im-
primam tanta cura Moriam ut in illa impressione
meipsum vicisse merito dici queam. Speramus hic 20
omnes tuum reditum, omnem tibi humanitatem
exhibituri. Salutat te Lachnerus socer et uxor,
Gertrudis uxor ac tota sodalitas nostra. Bene vale,
compater dilectissime.

        Basileae ex officina nostra xviiᵃ Iunii. 25
      Io. Frobennius, calcographus Basiliensis.

15. A Presentation Portrait

Erasmus and a young friend named Peter Gilles (Petrus Aegidius) decided to present More with a combined portrait of themselves, and commissioned the Dutch painter Quentin Matsys to execute it. The picture still exists, but is separated into its two parts.

The following piece is an extract from a letter written to Sir Thomas More from Antwerp in May 1517.

We had a hazardous landing near Boulogne, and the weather is stormy and unhealthy. Peter Gilles and I are having our portraits painted for you. Peter is unfortunately ill at the moment; I foolishly took some pills, which had such a disastrous effect that my appearance was quite altered, and the painter told me to come back when I felt better. Still no news of that horse! Peter and his wife send their good wishes.

Kalendis Maii ventis invalescentibus iamque etiam adversis medio noctis scaphula nautica non sine periculo in rupes quasdam eiecti sumus, in Galliam haud procul a Bolonia. Mox venti asperrimi, quos 5 reliquo itinere litus vicinum nobis exasperavit. Ii multos apud nos cynanche et pleuritide occiderunt et occidunt.

Petrus Aegidius et ego pingimur in eadem tabula: eam tibi dono brevi mittemus. Verum incidit 10 incommode quod reversus Petrum offenderim nescio-quo morbo graviter laborantem, nec citra periculum; unde nec adhuc satis revaluit. Nos belle valebamus

sed nescioquo modo medico venit in mentem ut
purgandae bili iuberet me pilulas aliquot sumere, et
quod ille stulte suasit, ego stultius feci. Iam pingi 15
coeperam; verum a pharmaco sumpto cum ad
pictorem redirem, negavit eundem esse vultum.
Dilata est igitur pictura in dies aliquot, donec fiam
paulo alacrior. . . . Scribam fusius intra mensem,
cum mittam tabellam. De equo nihil adhuc audio, 20
atqui nunc fuisset usui. Bene vale cum suavissima
coniuge liberisque dulcissimis. Petrus Aegidius una
cum Corneliola sua te tuamque plurimum salvere
iubet.

16. A Letter from the Bishop of Rochester

You have only to look at Holbein's portrait of
John Fisher, Bishop of Rochester, to realise that he
was a saint. He was also a man of great learning,
President of Queens' College, Cambridge, and
Chancellor of the University. In 1535, he and Sir
Thomas More suffered death for refusing to swear
to Henry VIII's recent Acts of Succession and
Supremacy. Though old and frail, he met his death
with supreme courage; his words to the Lieutenant
of the Tower before going out to execution show
his brave spirit.

He asked the Lieutenant to reach him his furred
tippet. 'Oh! my Lord,' said he, 'what need you be
now so careful of your health? Your time is short,
little more than half an hour.' 'I think none otherwise,' said the Bishop, 'but I pray you give me leave
to put on my furred tippet, to keep me warm for the
while until the very time of execution. For though

I have a very willing mind to die at this present, yet
will I not hinder my health in the meantime, not a
minute of an hour.'

EPISCOPUS ROFFENSIS DOMINO ERASMO S.P.

*I am glad to know that you arrived safely after
your dangerous voyage. It served you right for hurrying away
from me. More has not yet sent me the book presented to me
by Reuchlin. I shall write to Reuchlin when I have read it;
meanwhile please thank him for me.*

*Your New Testament is a most valuable and illuminating
work. The printer, however, has omitted several Greek words,
and even whole sentences. I have been working hard at my
Greek, but I wish you were here to teach me.*

Quantum erat molestum audire tuae navigationis
discrimen, tantum sane laetor quod salvus incolum-
isque evaseras. Iustum quidem erat ut poenam
dependeres tantae properationis tuae a me, apud
5 quem tutus ab omni iactatione pelagi quiescere
potuisti. Liber ille quo me scribis a Reuchlino
donatum, nondum ad me pervenit. Morus tuus
epistolam ad me misit, at librum adhuc suo more
detinet. Plurimum tibi devincior, Erasme, quum
10 ob alia tuae in me humanitatis studia, tum quod
tantopere anniteris ut Reuchlinus tam diligenter
meminerit mei. Eum animo toto complector; cui
interea donec perlecto libro ad eum scribam, significes
precor me gratias illi quantas animo cogitare possum,
15 habere maximas.

In Testamento Novo per te ad communem omnium
utilitatem traducto nemo qui sapit offendi potest,

quando non solum innumera in eo loca tua eruditione
plurimum illustrasti, verum etiam universo operi
integerrimam adhibuisti commentationem, ut nunc 20
multo quam ante gratius multoque iucundius ab
unoquoque et legi et intelligi possit.   At vereor sane
ne crebrius dormitarit impressor.   Nam ipse me
exercitans in lectione Pauli iuxta praeceptiones tuas,
repperi saepenumero dictiones Graecas illum omisisse, 25
ac nonnunquam sententias integras.   Tibi et istud
debeo, Erasme, quod conicere aliquousque possum,
ubi non omnino Latinis Graeca respondeant.   Utinam
aliquot menses licuisset habere te praeceptorem.

Felix vale ex Roffa.   30

Discipulus tuus Io. Roffensis.

17. A DESCRIPTION OF ZEALAND

Cuthbert Tunstall (1474–1559) was one of the
leaders of the Renaissance in England, and a friend
of Sir Thomas More, through whom he made the
acquaintance of Erasmus.   As a scholar, he studied
Greek, Hebrew, mathematics and law;   he was
frequently sent on embassies by Henry VIII to the
Emperor Charles V, and helped to negotiate the
Treaty of Cambrai in 1527;   he was Master of
the Rolls, and Bishop of London and Durham; as
President of the Council of the North he had the
difficult task of trying to keep peace with the Scots.
Like Erasmus, he was a man of moderation, and
while staunchly upholding Catholic doctrine was
opposed to the persecution of Protestants.   When he
was Bishop of London, he bought up at his own
expense all the copies he could find of Tyndale's

Translation of the Bible, and burnt them, to avoid
the necessity of persecuting his followers. They were
very grateful to him for supplying them with funds
to continue their work! He was friendly towards
Cranmer and the Protector Somerset, though not
agreeing with their reforming views, but after
Somerset's fall he was for a time deprived of his see
of Durham; Queen Mary reinstated him. He lost
his position again on Elizabeth's accession, because
he refused to take the Oath of Supremacy; he died
the following year at the age of eighty-five.

Erasmus entertained Tunstall and More at Brussels,
when they came as ambassadors to the Spanish king
in 1515. The embassy was protracted and unsuccessful, and this fact, in addition to the unpleasant climate
of Zealand which this letter describes, is enough to
account for Tunstall's mood of depression.

CUTHBERTUS TUNSTAL ERASMO S.P.D.

*1–43. The climate of Zealand has been so pestilential
that three of my servants fell sick of fever, and would have
died if I had not sent them away. Several members of the
Royal Court were also affected. In the towns, the evil-
smelling smoke of the peat fires penetrates everything. If
you walk in the country, the roads are deep in sticky mud,
and in order to reach the sea-walls, you have to cross countless
dykes, from which arises the foul odour of soaking flax.
Walking is, indeed, no recreation! Heavy drinking is the
only safeguard against this climate, men say; and, as you
know, I cannot compete in that line.*

Vix tandem Hispaniarum Rex in regnum navigavit,
et ego ex Selandia cum meis vix salvus redeo, usque
adeo taetro et plane pestilenti caeli illius infestatus
odore, ut multorum dierum inedia nondum febrem

accedentem omnino depulerim. Tres ex ministris, 5
atque his quidem commodioribus, ex febre prius
decubuerant quam illinc discessi: quos nisi con-
sulente medico caeli mutandi gratia statim amandas-
sem, omnes ante hunc extulissem diem. Neque haec
mea sors solius. Magna pars aulicorum aegrotabat: 10
habenda est Deo gratia, quod evaserit. Ex pur-
puratis afflicti certe aliquot; ita neminem non
vexatum dimisit illa insula.

Stygem arbitror non longe illinc abesse, ea est
aquarum nigritudo atque amarulentia. Si domi te 15
in oppido contines, undique ex vicinia glebularum
fumus (his namque vice lignorum utuntur) nares
opplet. Hae ex uliginoso et salso effossae solo,
quantumvis arefactae sole, dum ardent, fumum
reddunt in ipsa penetrantem praecordia, pectus, 20
nares, caput, omnia tentantem. Audivi ab indigenis
vestrates Hollandicas ex mitiore erutas solo thus olere
prae illis.

Quodsi fastidium oppidi levare obambulatione velis,
(id quod interim factitare consuevi), via ipsa, imbre 25
conspersa vel levi, tenacius omni visco pedem moratur
(nam ne in cuiusquam fundum aut pratum divertas
fossarum altitudo vetat); et ut ad aggeres in litore
exstructos arcendo mari tandem pervenias (quae una
iucunda est ambulatio), priusquam illo pervenias, 30
praeter sexcentas fossas tibi transeundum erit, quibus
linum macerant, quae foedo odore longe superant
omnem sentinam. Quantulum cloacae putent prae
illis! Ad haec praeter eiusmodi fossas itidem in
urbem reditus recreationem, si quam habuisti, tollit, 35

et tristem denuo domum remittit. Tota plane regio
duobus passibus est mari humilior in summo aestu;
et nisi aggeres arcerent, marinae beluae in comissantes
atque invicem propinantes incolas irrumperent. Ad
40 haec incommoda vitanda praesidium unicum esse
aiunt totos haurire congios; remedium certe mihi
gravius omni morbo. Nosti enim quam facile in eo
genere certaminis herbam porrigo.

44–60. *But why am I slandering this island, which has
so many admirable features? I do so for revenge, to work
off my irritation. But, seriously, I am thankful to have
returned to the mainland. When I am feeling better, I shall
crawl back to England, but I shall have to leave my sick
servants behind.*

*PS. One of my servants has died, and the recovery of
the others is doubtful.*

Sed quid facio, qui tam frugiferam insulam tamque
45 portuosam infamo, tacitis quae in laudationem eius
dici possent? Vis scire? Iuvat aliqua via me de illa
vindicare atque omnem ex eius taedio conceptam
bilem in illam ipsam effundere. Itaque nunc eius
encomium reticebo in vindictam. Sed, ut serio
50 tecum agam, gaudeo me tandem continenti redditum,
ubi caelum salubrius. Et ut patietur concussa
valetudo, paulatim adrepam in patriam: meos hic
relinquam gravius adhuc afflictos quam ut sequi
possent. Deum Optimum Maximum precor, ali-
55 quando convalescant.

Vale Brugis xviii Kal. Octobris.

Priusquam hanc obsignarem epistolam, unum ex

meis amiseram, cuius ego salutem omnibus meis
fortunis redemissem; cuius animae Deus sit propitius.
De reliquis adhuc dubia spes.   60

18. TRAVEL IN THE MIDDLE AGES

This letter, written to a familiar friend named Beat
Bild of Rheinau (Rhenanus), describes Erasmus'
journey down the Rhine from Basel to Louvain in
September 1518. It well illustrates his extreme
sensitiveness in the matter of climate, food and smells,
and shows us what a host of friends he had throughout western Europe. It is quite easy to trace out
his itinerary, though a detailed map will be required
to find some of the smaller places north-west of
Maastricht.

ERASMUS RHENANO SUO S.D.

[The summary of this letter is given in the form of
jottings from a diary.]

1–34. *1st day. Basel to Breisach. Voyage pleasant, but
rather hot. Lunch uneatable—poor service—smelly. Unknown village; supper in a hot and crowded room—guests
very noisy and tipsy; ate nothing and slept badly.*
*2nd day. Got up very early—voyage to Strasburg—fair
lunch. By road to Speyer—English horse in poor fettle.
Avoided the inn, and stayed the night with Maternus;
then two days with the Dean.*

Accipe, mi Beate, totam itineris mei tragico-
comoediam. Mollis etiamnum ac languidulus, ut
scis, Basileam relinquebam, ut qui nondum cum

caelo redissem in gratiam, cum tamdiu domi delituis-
5 sem, idque perpetuis laboribus distentus. Navigatio
fuit non inamoena, nisi quod circa meridiem solis
aestus erat submolestus. Brisaci pransi sumus, sed
ita ut nunquam insuavius. Nidor enecabat, tum
nidore graviores muscae. Desedimus plus semihoram
10 ad mensam otiosi, donec adornarent scilicet illi suas
epulas. Tandem nihil appositum est quod edi posset;
sordidae pultes, offae, salsamenta non semel recocta,
merae nauseae. Sub noctem eiecti sumus in vicum
quendam frigidum; cuius nomen nec libuit scire,
15 nec si sciam velim edere. Illic paene exstinctus sum.
In hypocausto non magno cenavimus plus opinor
sexaginta, promiscua hominum colluvies, idque ad
horam ferme decimam: O qui fetor, qui clamor,
praesertim ubi iam incaluerant vino! Et tamen ad
20 illorum clepsydras erat desidendum.

Mane multa adhuc nocte e stratis exturbamur
clamore nautarum. Ego et incenatus et insomnis
navim ingredior. Argentinam appulimus ante prandium ad horam ferme nonam; illic commodius
25 accepti sumus, praesertim Schurerio suppeditante
vinum. Illinc equis Spiram usque contendimus;
neque usquam militis umbram vidimus, cum rumor
atrocia sparsisset. Anglus equus plane defecit vixque
Spiram attigit; sic eum tractaverat sceleratus iste
30 faber, ut illi ambae aures ferro candenti inurerentur.
Spirae furtim me subduxi e diversorio, et ad Maternum
meum vicinum me recipio. Illic Decanus, vir doctus
et humanus, suaviter et comiter nos biduum accepit.
Hic forte fortuna Hermanum Buschium repperimus.

35–79. *5th day. Speyer to Mainz, via Worms, by coach; pleasant company. Stayed with one of the Canons.*
6th day. Mainz to Coblenz by boat. At Boppard, the incident of the learned customs officer—very flattering. Stayed with the Bishop's Secretary at Coblenz.
7th day. By boat to Cologne, arriving early. Went to Mass. Failed to hire a carriage; packed our bags and rode to Bedburg, to stay with the Count.

Illinc curru vectus sum Wormaciam, atque hinc 35
rursus Maguntiam. Forte in eundem currum in-
ciderat quidam Caesaris secretarius, Ulrichus cog-
nomento Farnbul. Is incredibili studio tum itinere
toto me observavit, tum Maguntiae, non passus
ingredi diversorium, ad aedes canonici cuiusdam 40
pertraxit: abeuntem ad navem deduxit. Navigatio
non fuit inamoena, nisi quod longior erat, nautarum
studio. Ad haec offendebat equorum paedor.

Ubi Popardiam appulimus, nosque, dum exploratur
navis, in ripa deambulabamus, nescio quis agnitum 45
me telonae prodidit. Telones est Christophorus, ni
fallor, Cinicampius, vulgato verbo Eschenfelder.
Incredibile dictu quam gestierit homo prae gaudio.
Pertrahit in aedes suas. In mensula inter syngraphas
telonicas iacebant Erasmi libelli. Beatum se clamitat, 50
advocat liberos, advocat uxorem, advocat amicos
omnes. Interim nautis vociferantibus mittit duos
vini cantharos, rursum vociferantibus mittit alteros,
pollicitus ubi redierint se illis vectigal remissurum,
qui talem virum sibi advexerint. Hinc officii gratia 55
comitatus est nos Confluentiam usque dominus
Ioannes Flaminius, virginibus sacris illic praefectus, vir
angelicae puritatis, iudicii sobrii sanique, doctrinae non

vulgaris. Confluentiae dominus Matthias, officialis
60 episcopi, nos domum suam rapit, homo iuvenis sed
moribus compositis; Latini sermonis exacte peritus,
tum iureconsultissimus. Illic cenatum est hilariter.

Apud Bonnam nos reliquit ille canonicus, vitans
urbem Coloniensem; quam et ipse vitare cupiebam,
65 sed minister cum equis eo praecesserat, neque quisquam erat in nave certus, cui de ministro revocando
negotium committere potuissem; et nautis diffidebam.
Mane itaque ante sextam Agrippinam appulimus die
Dominico, caelo iam pestilenti. Diversorium in-
70 gressus mando hospitii ministris de conducenda biga,
et cibum ad decimam parari iubeo. Audio sacrum,
prandium differtur. De biga non successit. Tenta-
tur de equo conducendo; nam mei erant inutiles.
Nihil succedit. Sensi id quod erat. Agebatur ut
75 illic haererem. Ego protinus iubeo meos adornari
equos, imponi alteram manticam, alteram hospiti
committo, et claudo meo equo ad Comitem Novae
Aquilae percurro; est autem iter horarum quinque.
Is agebat Bedburii.

Translation of next few lines.—I spent a very pleasant
five days with him; it was so quiet and peaceful that
I finished a good part of my New Testament at his
house. I wish you knew the man, Beatus. He is
young, but of a rare wisdom beyond his years; he is
sparing of speech, but, as Homer says of Menelaus, his
words are shrewd and sincere; he is well educated in
a variety of subjects, but does not show off his learning;
a genuinely frank and friendly person.

By this time I was restored to fairly sound health,
and very pleased with myself; I hoped I should be

in full vigour when I visited the Bishop of Liége, and returned to my friends in Brabant. What dinners, what greetings and conversations I looked forward to! If the autumn proved a mild one, I had determined to go to England, and accept what the King had so frequently offered. But how deceptive are men's hopes! Alas for the unexpected 'changes and chances of this mortal life'. From such dreams of happiness I was plunged into an abyss of misfortune.

A coach had been hired for the next day. Not wanting to bid me farewell the night before, the Count said he would see me in the morning before I left. During the night a violent storm of wind got up—it had begun on the previous day. Nevertheless I got up before midnight to write some notes for the Count; when seven o'clock came and he had not appeared, I asked that he should be aroused. He came, and in his shy and modest fashion asked me if it was my intention to leave in such unpleasant weather, saying that he was afraid for me. Then, my dear Beatus, some Jupiter or other, or evil spirit, took away not, as Hesiod says, half my mind, but all of it; he had already taken away one half, when I was foolish enough to go to Cologne. I only wish the Count had been more insistent in his advice, or that I had been more heedful of his polite and friendly warning. But the power of Fate swept me to my doom. What else can I call it?

80–116. *13th day. Started in stormy, wet weather, in an open carriage. Reached Aix very weary with the jolting over bad roads. Stayed at the Precentor's house; several Canons dining; very hungry, ate too much cold fish.*

14th day. Lunched with the Vice-Provost; no fresh fish except eels; I ate dried fish, half cooked. Went to the inn to make arrangements with the coachman; had a fire

4

*lit.   Tried to refuse invitation to supper;   returned to the
Precentor's, feeling shivery.*

80   Conscendo bigam non tectam, flante vento
                quantus altis montibus
        Frangit trementes ilices.

Auster erat, neque quicquam praeter meras pestes
spirabat.   Ego mihi vestibus probe tectus videbar,
85 sed ille violentia sua nihil non penetrabat.   Successit
sub noctem pluviola, vento suo pestilentior.   Venio
Aquisgranum lassulus ob quassationem bigae, quae
mihi in via saxis constrata tam erat gravis, ut equo
quamlibet claudo maluerim insidere.   Hic per can-
90 onicum quendam, cui me Comes commendarat,
rapior e diversorio ad aedes cantoris.   Ibi ex more convivium agitabant aliquot canonici.   Mihi prandium
tenuissimum acuerat stomachum;   sed apud hos
tum nihil erat praeter carpas, easque frigidas.
95 Expleo me.   Cum in multam noctem (nam serius
accubuerant) cena proferretur fabulis, ego petita
venia cubitum abeo, quod proxima nocte minimum
dormieram.
        Postridie pertrahor ad aedes Vicepraepositi; nam
100 ad illum redierat periodus.   Ibi cum praeter anguil-
lam nihil erat piscium,—nimirum tempestas fuerat
in culpa, cum ipse sit alioqui splendidus convivator
—expleo me pisce durato ventis, quem a baculo quo
contunditur Germani 'stockfisch' vocant: nam eo
105 alioqui satis delector; sed comperi partem huius
adhuc crudam fuisse.   A prandio, quoniam caelum

erat pestilentissimum, in diversorium me confero.
Iubeo excitari foculum. Confabulatur mecum canonicus ille, vir humanissimus, ferme sesquihoram.
Deinde pactus cum auriga de manticis, rursus 110
invitor ad cenam. Excuso, non proficio. Apparatus
tum erat praelautus, sed mihi frustra. Ubi con-
fovissem stomachum sorbitiuncula, domum me confero; dormiebam enim apud cantorem. Egredior;
ibi corpus inane mire ad nocturnum caelum inhorruit. 115
Nox gravis fuit.

117–164. 15*th day.* Aix to Tongres, via Maastricht.
   Feeling very unwell; uncomfortable journey on horseback.
16*th day.* Hired a carriage, but decided to ride on one of
   the horses; came over faint, and had to enter the carriage;
   managed to reach Tènes, *six miles.*
17*th day.* Tènes to Louvain by coach.

Postridie mane rursus hausta cervisiola tepida cum
paucis micis panis, equum conscendo morbidum et
claudum; quo fuit incommodior equitatio. Iam
sic affectus eram ut magis conveniret lecto confoveri 120
quam equo insidere. Sed ea regio non parum habet
rusticitatis, commoditatis aut elegantiae minimum, et
illic mihi ne valere quidem satis esset commodum,
nedum aegrotare; quo magis libebat effugere.
Latronum periculum (nam ibi summum erat) aut 125
certe metum extudit morbi molestia. Confectis eo
cursu quattuor passuum milibus perventum est ad
Mosae Traiectum. Illic sorbitiuncula utcunque
confoto stomacho, rursus inscensis equis Tongros
adeo. Id oppidum abest tribus milibus passuum. 130

Haec postrema equitatio mihi longe gravissima fuit.
Incommodus incessus equi mire torquebat renes.
Tolerabilius ambulabam pedibus, sed metuebam
sudorem, et periculum erat ne nox in agris nos
135 occupasset; itaque incredibili totius corporis cruciatu
Tongros pervenio.

Iam ob inediam ac laborem inediae additum
omnes corporis nervi defecerant; adeo ut nec firmus
esset status aut incessus. Lingua—nam ea valebat—
140 dissimulabam morbi magnitudinem. Hic cervisiaria
sorbitiuncula foto stomacho cubitum eo. Mane iubeo
conduci bigam tectam. Mihi visum est ob silices
equo insidere, donec ad terrenam viam esset ventum.
Conscendo maiorem equum, quod is commodius iret
145 per saxa et pedibus certioribus. Vix conscenderam,
contactus caelo frigido sentio oboriri glaucoma, posco
pallium. Sed mox syncopis successit. Vel manu
contacta poteram excitari. Ibi meus Ioannes cum
ceteris astantibus passi sunt in equo sedentem mea
150 sponte expergisci. Experrectus bigam conscendo.

Iam eramus vicini oppido divi Trudonis. Rursus
inscendo equum, ne biga vectus viderer aegrotus.
Rursus caelo vespertino offensus nauseo, sed citra
syncopim. Offero duplum pretium bigario, ut me
155 postridie vehat usque ad Tenas. Id oppidum abest a
Tongris sex milibus passuum. Accipit condicionem.
Hic hospes mihi notus narrat quam graviter tulerit
Episcopus Leodiensis, quod se insalutato discessissem
Basileam petens. Confoto stomacho sorbitiuncula eo
160 cubitum. Hic forte quadrigam nactus, quae Lovanium
peteret (aberat autem sex milibus passuum), in eam

me conicio. Incredibili molestia vectus sum, ac paene intolerabili, sed tamen eo die ad horam septimam pervenimus Lovanium.

19. THE PLAGUE OR NOT THE PLAGUE?

The illness which Erasmus contracted during his long journey to Louvain so filled his thoughts that he wrote a description of it, with varying amounts of detail, to half a dozen of his friends. This letter, dated October 23, 1518, to Bishop Fisher of Rochester, starts with a brief summary of the journey, in which he manages to include a passing hit at his opponents, the monks. Then follows an account of his illness. Another letter gives much more detail. Erasmus called in all the physicians and surgeons in Louvain, some of whom said that his disease was not the plague, while others, when told of the ulcers, declared that it was, and refused to visit him again. In the end, Erasmus says he dispensed with doctors altogether, and 'trusted to Christ as his physician'. He cured himself in three days by a diet of chicken-broth and wine. It is not easy to reconcile this with line 32 of this letter, where he says he had already been in the doctors' hands for six weeks.

1–21. *This has been a trying summer for me. I was not well when I left Basel, but had recovered somewhat by the time I reached Bedburg. The Count is a model youth, and well educated. What a contrast to the monks and priests! The customs officer at Boppard is another example, and I receive letters from laymen all over Europe, showing the true Christian spirit.*

S.P., reverende Praesul. Hic annus pulchre exercuit Erasmum tuum, et itio et reditio fuit

difficillima partim ob aestum, qui in Germania
fuit intolerabilis, partim ob ventos pestilentissimos.
5 Languidulus adhuc reliqueram Basileam: tamen
paulatim ita convalueram ut mihi satis placerem, ubi
venissem ad Comitem Novae Aquilae. Hunc repperi
in Arce Bedburiensi quattuor milibus passuum citra
Coloniam. Iuvenis est antiqua nobilitate, pauci-
10 loquus, sobrius, moribus modestissimis ac plane
sanctis, non una in disciplina doctus. O vices turpiter
commutatas, si sacerdotes et monachi ventri gulaeque
serviunt, militibus bonos mores ac bonas litteras
amplectentibus! Offendi et Bobardiae telonem qui
15 exiliit prae gaudio, beatum se clamitans quod
Erasmum videre contigisset. Nihil officii non ex-
hibuit. Inter syngraphas telonicas libellos Erasmi
ostendit. Scribunt ad me ex Norenberga, ex
Bohemia, ex Ungaria, ex Polonia litteras Christum
20 spirantes; sed profani fere omnes. Soli monachi et
theologi quidam horum similes sycophantas agunt.

22–44. *Oh! the changes and chances of this life! When
I reached Louvain, I was in a very feeble state. I was
suffering from ulcers, brought on by riding. The surgeons,
in whose hands I have been for six weeks, declared that I had
the plague, but I refused to believe them. I shall bear my
afflictions with calmness, trusting to the protection of Christ.*

Sed ut ad rem, sperabam fore ut hoc autumno
laetus laetos reviserem vos; sed o vices subitas rerum
humanarum! Simul atque Comitem reliqui, repente
25 in extremum exitium praecipitatus sum. Praeter
animum nihil supererat vitae. Semivivus delatus sum

Lovanium, omnibus viribus destitutus. Habebam
tria ulcera, unum ingens sub laeva coxa, quod
equitatione quoque fuit exacerbatum, alterum in
laevo inguine, tertium in tergo. Uterque chirurgus 30
pestem esse asseveravit, et adhuc asseverat. Mihi
non libuit credere. Iam sextam hebdomadem mihi
cum chirurgis res est, periculosissimo hominum
genere, ac domi desideo. Quis credidisset hoc
corpusculum tot profectionibus, tot morbis, tot 35
laboribus, tot curis suffecturum fuisse? Dabit aliquando Christus Opt. Max. his prosperiora. Quamquam quicquid ille nos ferre voluerit, feremus aequo
animo; modo—quod speramus illius freti bonitate—
membrum hoc suum, licet languidum, non sinat a 40
suo corpore revelli. Ille nobis vita, si morimur; ille
praesidium, si vivimus. Bene vale, praesulum integerrime, et Erasmum clientulum, ut soles, ama.

Lovanii x Kalend. Nov.

20. In Praise of Henry VIII

Sir Henry Guildford (1489–1532) received two
letters from Erasmus in 1519, both in praise of
Henry VIII. Erasmus was wise in his choice of a
correspondent, because Sir Henry was a great
favourite of the King throughout his life. Besides
being a soldier, he seems to have been a bit of an
actor. We are told that in 1510 he was one of a
company of twelve courtiers who gave a performance
of *Robin Hood and his Merry Men*, for the amusement
of the Queen; and in 1513 the victory of Tournai
was celebrated by an 'interlude', which he organised,

and in which he took a part. He had been the King's
Standard-bearer during the war, and in 1515 he was
appointed Master of the Horse, by which title Erasmus
here addresses him. He was present at the Field of
the Cloth of Gold (1520) and during Henry's sub-
sequent meeting with the Emperor at Gravelines.
Later, as Controller of the Royal Household, he had
to make the arrangements for the entertainment of
Cardinal Campeggio, who had come from the Pope
in the matter of Henry's divorce from Catherine of
Aragon. In addition to his Court duties, he found
time to act as a Justice of the Peace, and as Sheriff
for the County of Kent; through royal favour he
amassed a considerable fortune. His portrait, by
Holbein, is in Windsor Castle.

In this letter, as in the previous letter to the Bishop
of Rochester, Erasmus contrasts the ignorance and
worldliness of the clergy with the culture to be found
among laymen. Though this eulogy of the young
English King and his Court springs from genuine
conviction, Erasmus certainly had hopes that it would
bear fruit in the form of financial assistance.

D. HENRICO GULDEFORDO, PRAEFECTO REI EQUESTRIS
REGIS ANGLIAE, ERAS. S.P.

1–32. *My friends tell me that you are well-disposed
towards me because of my labours in the cause of learning.
The world is waking up, in spite of bitter and ignorant
opposition. What a change has taken place! Learning was
once the province of the Church; now it is to be found
among kings and courtiers, especially in the English Court.
The Church has fallen from its high ideals.*

Vir clarissime, multorum sermone cognosco quam
amico sis in nos animo, sive scintillas istius bene-

volentiae ex meis lucubrationibus concepisti, sive ex
D. Ioannis Coleti ceterorumque amicorum hausisti
sermone. Tu me diligis quod vere talem esse credas 5
qualem illi praedicaverunt. Ego te vicissim amo
quod toto pectore virtuti, quod honestis studiis
faveas, quando horum gratia mihi quoque faves:
non quod his praeditus sim, sed quod tibi persuasum
est his praeditum esse me. Certe recta studia, 10
praesertim ea quae ad veram faciunt pietatem,
provehere semper conatus sum, sed utinam perinde
feliciter ac sedulo. Mundus resipiscit velut ex
altissimo somno expergiscens; et tamen pertinacibus
animis adhuc repugnant quidam, veterem inscitiam 15
suam manibus pedibusque ac mordicus etiam
retinentes. Sed hos pudebit amentiae suae, si
viderint summos reges ac regum proceres amplecti,
fovere, tueri meliores literas.

O miras rerum humanarum vicissitudines! Olim 20
literarum ardor penes religionis professores erat;
nunc illis magna ex parte ventri luxui pecuniaeque
vacantibus, amor eruditionis ad principes profanos
ac proceres aulicos demigrat. Nam quae schola,
quod monasterium usquam tam multos habet 25
insigni probitate doctrinaque praeditos quam vestra
habet aula? An non optimo iure nos nostri
pudeat? Sacerdotum ac theologorum convivia
madent vinolentia, scurrilibus opplentur iocis,
tumultu parum sobrio perstrepunt, virulentis ob- 30
trectationibus scatent: et ad principum mensas
modeste disputatur de iis quae ad eruditionem ac
pietatem faciunt.

33–60. I once shrank from Court life, but now I would gladly move with all my belongings to such a Court as yours, were it not for my age and ill-health. Who will now say that learning makes kings effeminate? Where is there a finer soldier or a better ruler than Henry VIII? A Golden Age is beginning, though I shall not live to enjoy it. I return your affection, and am grateful for your services to me. I send my good wishes to your Lady Mother.

Olim otii literarumque dulcedine captus ab aulis
35 regum abhorrebam; at in talem aulam vel cum tota
supellectile, quae fere chartacea est, liberet im-
migrare, ni valetudinis imbecillitas et aetas iam
ingravescens dissuaderet. Ubi nunc sunt qui iactitant
principum vigori officere literarum cognitionem?
40 Quis Henrico octavo vel in bellicis rebus dexterior,
vel in condendis legibus cordatior, vel in consiliis
oculatior, vel in coercenda scelerum licentia vigil-
antior, vel in deligendis magistratibus atque officiis
diligentior, vel in conciliandis foedere regibus
45 efficacior? Equidem aureum quoddam saeculum
exoriri video, quo mihi fortassis non continget frui,
quippe qui iam ad fabulae meae catastrophen
accedam; gratulor tamen orbi, gratulor iuvenibus, in
quorum animis ob officiorum memoriam utcumque
50 superstes erit Erasmus.

Sed ut finiam, ornatissime Henrice, redamo te
amantem, proque officiis in me tuis non vulgaribus
hoc maiorem habeo gratiam, quod ea praestiteris
nullo unquam a me lacessitus officio. Generosae
55 dominae matri tuae, mihi uno atque altero colloquio
cognitae, precor omnia laeta prosperaque. Istum

animum tibi, te nobis servet Opt. Max. Iesus.   Hunc
Erasmum pergat tua nobilitas inter clientulos ponere,
studio certe nulli cessurum.

Antuuerpiae.   Id. Maii.   Anno MDXIX.   60
Erasmus Roterodamus ex animo tuus.

21. ENGLISH HOUSES

This letter was written to John Francis, physician
to Cardinal Wolsey, and one of the founders, together
with Linacre, of the Royal College of Physicians in
1518; Wolsey himself was the chief supporter of the
Royal College.   The date of this letter is uncertain.

ERASMUS ROTERODAMUS FRANCISCO CARDINALIS
EBORACENSIS MEDICO S.D.

1–22. *I have often wondered why England suffers so
continually from the plague.   There are certain changes that
I think would be beneficial:* (a) *the rooms are not properly
ventilated, and the lattice windows admit unhealthy draughts;*
(b) *the rushes on the floors remain undisturbed for long periods,
and become offensive and insanitary.*

Frequenter et admirari et dolere soleo, qui fiat ut
Britannia tot iam annis assidua pestilentia vexetur,
praesertim sudore letali, quod malum paene videtur
habere peculiare. Legimus civitatem a diutina
pestilentia liberatam, consilio philosophi mutatis   5
aedificiis.   Aut me fallit animus, aut simili ratione
liberari possit Anglia.

Primum quam caeli partem spectent fenestrae
ostiave nihil habent pensi: deinde sic fere constructa

10 sunt conclavia, ut nequaquam sint perflabilia, quod
inprimis admonet Galenus. Tum magnam parietis
partem habent vitreis tessellis pellucidam, quae sic
admittunt lumen ut ventos excludant, et tamen per
rimulas admittunt auram illam colatam, aliquanto
15 pestilentiorem, ibi diu quiescentem. Tum sola fere
strata sunt argilla, tum scirpis palustribus, qui
subinde sic renovantur ut fundamentum maneat
aliquoties annos viginti, sub se fovens sputa, vomitus,
proiectam cervisiam et piscium reliquias, aliasque
20 sordes non nominandas. Hinc mutato caelo vapor
quidam exhalatur, mea sententia minime salubris
humano corpori.

23–42. *I recommend* (a) *the abolition of the use of rushes,
and* (b) *the better construction of windows, so that they can
be either entirely open or entirely shut: I myself have always
felt ill upon entering an unventilated room;* (c) *the people
should be more moderate in eating, particularly of salted
foods;* (d) *the authorities should keep the roads cleaner.*

Adde quod Anglia non solum undique circumfusa
est mari, verum etiam multis in locis palustris est
25 salsisque fluminibus intersecta; ne quid dicam
interim de salsamentis, quibus vulgus mirum in
modum delectatur. Confiderem insulam fore multo
salubriorem si scirporum usus tolleretur; tum si sic
exstruerentur cubicula, ut duobus aut tribus lateribus
30 paterent caelo; fenestris omnibus vitreis ita confectis,
ut totae possent aperiri, totae claudi, et sic claudi
ut non pateret per hiantes rimas aditus ventis noxiis.
Siquidem ut aliquando salutiferum est admittere

:aelum, ita nonnunquam salutiferum est excludere.
Ridet vulgus si quis offenditur caelo nubiloso. Ego 35
et ante annos triginta, si fueram ingressus cubiculum
in quo mensibus aliquot nemo versatus esset, ilico in-
cipiebam febricitare. Conferret huc si vulgo parcior
victus persuaderi posset ac salsamentorum moderatior
usus; tum si publica cura demandaretur aedilibus, 40
ut viae mundiores essent a caeno, curarentur et ea
quae civitati vicina essent.

*43–54. You will wonder that I have nothing better to do
than to offer you advice on a matter in which your own
knowledge probably exceeds mine, but I have a great affection
for hospitable England. I should have written to the
Cardinal, but I know how busy he is.*

Ridebis, scio, otium meum, qui his de rebus
sollicitus sim. Faveo regioni quae mihi tam diu
praebuit hospitium, et in qua libens finiam quod 45
superest aevi, si liceat. Nec dubito quin tu haec pro
tua prudentia rectius noris; libuit tamen admonere,
ut, si meum iudicium cum tuo consentiat, haec viris
principibus persuadeas. Haec enim olim regum
cura consuevit esse. Scripsissem perlibenter reverend- 50
issimo domino Cardinali; sed nec otium erat nec
argumentum, nec ignoro quibus ille negotiis di-
stringatur. Bene vale, vir humanissime, cui debeo
plurimum.

22. AN EXPLOSION AT BASEL

This letter describes the devastating effects of an
explosion of gunpowder, which occurred in Basel in

September 1526. It is addressed to the principal o
a college in Louvain. Erasmus lived in the University
of Louvain for some years, before going to Basel in
1521, in order to be near his printer, John Froben.
When the Reformation began to cause religious dis-
turbances there, he had to leave the city for some
time, but returned a year before his death in 1536.

ERASMUS ROTERODAMUS NICOLAO VARIO MARVILLANO S.

*1–23. Some news it is hardly safe for me to write, but
here is a strange incident which took place in Basel recently.
I had been strolling in the garden, as is my custom in the
afternoon, and had just begun to do some translation in the
summer-house, when I saw the windows shaking. Then there
were flashes, and I looked out to see if a thunderstorm was
brewing. Soon there was a dull report and more flashes,
followed by a terrible crash.*

*[My mind went back to a violent thunderstorm in Bologna,
when three nuns were killed.]*

Multa quidem nova cotidie nobis gignit hic Africa
nostra, Nicolae carissime; sed quaedam eius sunt
generis, ut nec tibi gratum arbitrer futurum legere
nec mihi tutum scribere. Quod nuper accidit accipe.
5 A.d. duodecimum Calendas Octobres, evocatus
amoenitate caeli, secesseram in hortum, quem Ioannes
Frobenius satis amplum et elegantem meo com-
mercatus est hortatu. Nam ibi soleo pomeridianis
aliquot horis vel somnum obrepentem arcere vel
10 assiduitatis taedium fallere, si quando invitat aeris
temperies. Post deambulatiunculam conscenderam
domunculam hortensem, iamque coeperam aliquid ex
Chrysostomo vertere, cum interim vitreas fenestras

ferit fulmen, sed tacitum ac lene. Primum suspicabar
oculorum esse errorem. Cum rursus semel atque 15
iterum effulsisset, demiror ac prospicio si se vertisset
caelum, contractisque nubibus pluviam ac tem-
pestatem minaretur. Ubi nihil video periculi, ad
librum redeo. Mox auditur sonitus, sed obtusior.
Paulo post emicat plus fulgoris, et audio fragorem 20
horribilem, cuiusmodi fere crepitus audiri solet, si
quando fulminis ictus impegit se vehementius in
aliquid solidum.

Translation of the next few lines.—When I was living
in Florence, at the time when Pope Julius was hurling
his thunders and lightning against Bologna, there was
a violent thunderstorm lasting nearly all day, and a
great quantity of rain fell. When a horrible crash
was heard, I retired in terror, and went back to the
others. 'Either my judgment is at fault,' I said, 'or
after that noise you will hear some sad news.' And,
sure enough, not long afterwards there came a surgeon,
telling us that three women had been struck in a
nunnery; one had died almost at once, the second
was at the point of death, and the third so seriously
injured that he said there was no hope of her recovery.

24–42. *Looking out, I saw an ash-coloured cloud of a very
strange shape. One of the servants then rushed up, bidding
me return to the house. He said that the whole city was in
a state of armed confusion. The citizens always stand to
arms when there is a fire, and the streets are hardly safe.
I met many armed men on my way home.*

Ad similem itaque sonitum surrexi et prospicio
quae sit caeli facies. Ad laevam erat serenitas, ad 25
dextram conspicio novam nubis speciem, velut e

terra sese proferentis in sublime, colore propemodum
cinericio, cuius cacumen velut inflexum sese de-
mittebat. Dixisses scopulum quempiam esse vertice
30 nutantem in mare. Quo contemplor attentius, hoc
minus videbatur nubi similis. Dum ad hoc spectaculum stupeo, accurrit famulorum unus quem domi
reliqueram, anhelus, admonens ut subito me domum
recipiam; civitatem armatam in tumultu esse. Nam
35 is mos est huic reipublicae, ut sicubi fuerit exortum
incendium, confestim armati procurrant ad tuendas
portas ac moenia. Nec satis tutum est armatis
occurrere; ferrum enim addit ferociam animis,
praesertim ubi nihil est periculi. Hortus autem in
40 quo studebam erat pone moenia. Recurro domum,
multis obviis armatis.

42–66. *What had happened was this.* *One of the towers
on the wall was used as a powder magazine, and the barrels
had been carelessly placed at the bottom instead of the top.
A flash of lightning had touched off all this powder, and the
force of the explosion had split the tower into four equal parts,
demolishing houses over a wide area.*

Aliquanto post rem totam didicimus, quae sic habebat. Paucis ante diebus in unam turrim earum quibus
moenia ex intervallis muniuntur, delata fuerant
45 aliquot vasa pulveris bombardici. Ea cum magistratus iussisset reponi in summa camera turris,
nescioquorum incuria reposita sunt in imam turrim.
Quod si vis pulveris in summo fuisset, tectum modo
sustulisset in aera, reliquis innocuis. Ac miro casu
50 per rimas illas speculatorias fulmen illapsum attigit

pulverem, moxque vasa omnia corripuit incendium.
Primum impetus incendii tentavit an esset oneri
ferendo possetque totam molem in altum tollere.
Idque testantur qui viderunt turrim iuxta partes imas
hiantem semel atque iterum, sed rursus in se 55
coeuntem. Ubi vis ignis sensit molem esse graviorem
quam ut totam posset subvehere, eo conatu relicto
totam turrim in quattuor partes immani crepitu
dissecuit, sed tanta aequalitate ut amussi geometrica
factum videri posset, ac per aera aliam alio sparsit. 60
Ipse pulvis accensus in altum se recepit, qui flamma
consumpta cinericiae nubis praebebat speciem.
Vidisses immania fragmenta turris, avium ritu,
volitare per aera; quaedam ad ducentos passus
deferri, qua dabatur liberum aeris spatium; alia 65
civium domos longo tractu demoliri.

*67–80. Some small 'council houses' were the worst
sufferers. The crash was so sudden and violent that many
people thought the end of the world had come. There were
several casualties in the fields outside, twelve killed and
fourteen seriously injured. Some thought the disaster was
an omen; I think it merely shows the thoughtlessness of those
who should have known better.*

Non procul a turri magistratus curarat exstruendas
aediculas quasdam. Hae lateris unius impetum
excepere. Tantus autem erat fragor tamque subitus,
ut qui erant in propinquo putarent rupto caelo 70
mundum in chaos abiturum. Nec ridiculum putabatur quod vulgo dici solet: 'Quid si caelum ruat?'
In agris multi sunt ruina oppressi, multi sic membris

vel truncati vel afflicti ut miserandum spectaculum
75 praeberent obviis: e quibus aiunt exstinctos numero
duodecim, misere vexatos quattuordecim. Sunt qui
credant hoc ostento quiddam portendi in futurum;
ego nihil aliud arbitror significari quam incogitan-
tiam eorum qui casum eum non adeo rarum non
80 praecaverint.

23. Erasmus' 'Apologia pro vita sua'

In July 1514 Erasmus left England after his third
and longest visit, and was staying for a few days with
his patron, Lord Mountjoy, who was the Governor
of Hammes Castle, an important military stronghold
in the English dominion of Calais. Here he received
a letter, dispatched the previous Easter, from an old
friend of his, who had been with him in the monastery
of Steyn during those miserable eight years before he
left to become secretary to the Bishop of Cambrai.
This friend, Servatius Rogerus, had now risen to be
Prior of Steyn, and wrote reproaching Erasmus for
having abandoned the monastic life, and even the
dress of his order, and strongly urging him to return
to the monastery. Erasmus wrote a long and carefully reasoned reply, explaining why a monk's life was
impossible for him, and why he had ceased to wear
the monastic habit; he also justified his belief that
he had made the best use of his literary talents by
remaining free.

The Life of Erasmus in the Introduction should be
read in conjunction with this letter.

1–26. *Your letter has at last reached me. I shall reply
briefly to the most important points in it. I never planned*

*to change my way of life, but I was forced into it by
my guardians, though I knew that I was unsuited for it.
My constitution could not stand the rigours of a monastery.
You mention the year of probation, but it is absurd to expect
a boy of seventeen to know his own mind in a year.*

Humanissime pater, literae tuae per plurimorum
iactatae manus tandem ad me quoque pervenerunt
iam Angliam egressum; quae mihi sane voluptatem
incredibilem attulerunt, quod veterem illum tuum in
me animum adhuc spirant.   Paucis autem respondeo,   5
utpote ex itinere iam scribens, et ad ea potissimum
quae tu scribis ad rem maxime pertinere.

Nunquam mihi fuit consilium vel vitae genus vel
cultum mutare, non quod probarem, sed ne cui
scandalo essem.   Scis enim me ad id vitae genus 10
tutorum pertinacia et aliorum improbis hortatibus
adactum esse magis quam inductum: tum Cornelii
Woerdeni conviciis et pudore quodam puerili fuisse
retentum, cum intellegerem mihi hoc vitae genus
haudquaquam aptum esse;   nam non omnibus 15
congruunt omnia.   Ieiuniorum semper impatiens fui,
idque peculiari quadam corporis ratione.   Semel
excitatus e somno nunquam potui redormiscere nisi
post horas aliquot.   Ad literas tantum rapiebatur
animus, quarum illic nullus usus.   20

At obiciet mihi aliquis annum probationis (ut
vocant) et aetatem maturam.   Ridiculum.   Quasi
quis postulet ut puer anno decimo septimo, maxime
in literis educatus, norit se ipsum, quod magnum
est etiam in sene, aut anno uno id discere potuerit 25
quod multi cani nondum intellegunt.

27–44. My aim was to choose the best career for myself, and I think I have succeeded. I have enjoyed the society of learned and Christian men; my writings have benefited many; I care nothing for money, fame, or pleasure. If I rejoined you, all would despise me. Besides, your whole way of life is abhorrent to me.

Hoc igitur interim spectavi, in quo vitae genere minime malus essem, atque id sane me assecutum puto. Vixi interim inter sobrios, vixi in studiis
30 literarum, quae me a multis vitiis avocaverunt. Licuit consuetudinem habere cum viris vere Christum sapientibus, quorum colloquio factus sum melior. Nihil enim iam iacto de libris meis, quos fortasse vos contemnitis. At multi fatentur se redditos eorum
35 lectione non solum eruditiores verum etiam meliores. Pecuniae studium nunquam me attigit. Famae gloria nec tantillum tangor. Voluptatibus, etsi quondam fui inclinatus, nunquam servivi. Crapulam et ebrietatem semper horrui fugique. Quoties autem
40 cogitabam de repetendo vestro contubernio, succurrebat invidia multorum, contemptus omnium, colloquia quam frigida, quam inepta, convivia quam laica; denique tota vitae ratio, cui si detraxeris caerimonias, non video quid relinquas expetendum.

45–68. Finally, my health is so weak that I have to be careful what I eat and drink. For years I have suffered from 'the stone'. You may say that it would be blessed to die among the brethren—a fallacious argument. You think that the Christian religion is a matter of dress and ritual; I venture to say that these have been destructive of true Christian piety.

Postremo succurrebat corporis imbecillitas, quae 45
iam aetate et morbis et laboribus aucta est; quae
facit ut nec vobis satisfacturus essem et me ipsum
occiderem. Iam annis aliquot obnoxius sum calculo,
gravi sane malo et capitali. Iam annis aliquot
nihil bibo nisi vinum, neque quodvis vinum, idque 50
cogente morbo. Non fero quemvis cibum, nec
caelum quidem quodlibet. Nam morbus hic facile
recurrens maximam postulat vitae moderationem;
et novi caelum Hollandicum, novi victus vestri
rationem, ut de moribus nihil dicam. Itaque si 55
redissem, nihil aliud fuissem assecutus nisi quod
vobis molestiam attulissem et mihi mortem.

Sed tu forsitan bonam felicitatis partem existimes
inter confratres emori. At fallit et imponit ista
persuasio non solum tibi verum etiam propemodum 60
universis. In loco, in cultu, in victu, in caerimoniolis
quibusdam Christum et pietatem collocamus. Actum
putamus de illo qui vestem albam commutarit in
nigram, aut qui cucullum pileo verterit, qui locum
subinde mutet. Ausim illud dicere, magnam 65
Christianae pietatis perniciem ex istis quas vocant
religionibus exortam esse, tametsi pio studio primum
inductae sunt.

69–94. *You wish me to have a settled home for my old
age. But many great men of antiquity have been wanderers,
including Paul and Jerome. I do not compare myself with
these, but when I have moved about, it has been for my health
or my work. I have been welcomed all over Europe; at
Rome, Cardinals and Pope have treated me as a brother, not
because I was wealthy or ambitious, but because I was a
scholar.*

Vis me sedem stabilem figere, quod ipsa etiam
70 suadet senectus. At laudatur Solonis, Pythagorae
Platonisque peregrinatio. Vagabantur et Apostoli,
praecipue Paulus. Divus Hieronymus etiam monachus nunc Romae est, nunc in Syria, nunc in
Antiochia, nunc alibi atque alibi; et canus etiam
75 sacras persequitur literas.

At non sum cum hoc conferendus, fateor; sed
tamen nunquam mutavi locum, nisi vel peste cogente,
vel studii causa vel valetudinis, et ubicunque vixi
(dicam enim de me ipso fortassis arrogantius, sed
80 tamen vere), probatus sum a probatissimis et
laudatus a laudatissimis. Nec ulla est regio, nec
Hispania, nec Italia, nec Germania, nec Gallia, nec
Anglia, nec Scotia, quae me ad suum non invitet
hospitium. Et si non probor ab omnibus (quod
85 nec studeo), certe primis omnium placeo.

Romae nullus erat Cardinalis qui non me tanquam
fratrem acciperet, cum ipse nihil tale ambirem;
praecipue vero Cardinalis Grimanus, et hic ipse qui
nunc Pontifex Maximus est, ut ne dicam de episcopis,
90 archidiaconis et viris eruditis. Atque hic honos non
tribuebatur opibus, quas etiam nunc non habeo nec
desidero; non ambitioni, a qua semper fui alienissi-
mus; sed literis duntaxat, quas nostrates rident, Itali
adorant.

95–125. *In England the bishops value my society. The
King writes me friendly letters, and speaks of me with honour
and affection. The Queen wanted me to be her tutor. I
could have had as many livings as I wished, but I preferred
my independence. The Archbishop of Canterbury gave me a*

living, and at my request changed it for a pension. He, as well as other bishops, has made me many gifts of money. Lord Mountjoy grants me an annual pension.

In Anglia nullus est episcopus qui non gaudeat a 95 me salutari, qui non cupiat me convivam, qui nolit domesticum. Rex ipse paulo ante patris obitum, cum essem in Italia, scripsit ad me suapte manu literas amantissimas, nunc quoque saepe sic de me loquitur ut nemo honorificentius, nemo amantius; 100 et quoties eum saluto, blandissime complectitur et oculis amicissimis obtuetur, ut intellegas eum non minus bene de me sentire quam loqui. Et saepe mandavit suo eleemosynario ut mihi de sacerdotio prospiceret. Regina conata est me sibi praeceptorem 105 adsciscere. Nemo est qui nesciat me, si vel paucos menses velim in aula regis vivere, quantum libeat sacerdotiorum mihi accumulaturum; sed ego huic otio meo et studiorum laboribus omnia posthabeo.

Cantuariensis Archiepiscopus, totius Angliae primas 110 et regni huius Cancellarius, vir doctus et probus, me sic amplectitur ut, si pater esset aut frater, non posset amantius. Et ut intellegas hoc eum ex animo facere, dedit mihi sacerdotium centum ferme nobilium, quod postea volente me in pensionem centum 115 coronatorum mutavit, ex mea resignatione; ad haec dedit dono supra quadringentos nobiles his pauculis annis, idque nihil unquam petenti. Dedit uno die nobiles centum et quinquaginta. Ab aliis episcopis supra centum nobiles accepi gratuita liberalitate 120 oblatos. Dominus Montioius, huius regni baro, quondam meus discipulus, dat annue mihi pensionem

centum coronatorum. Rex et episcopus Lincolniensis, qui nunc per regem omnia potest, magnifice
125 multa promittunt.

*126–154. Oxford and Cambridge both desire to have me,
and I have found there true religion. The Dean of St Paul's
is one of my closest friends, and I could name many others.
My writings, such as the* Adagia, *have proved useful to
many. I have edited the letters of St Jerome and the New
Testament, and have begun a Commentary on St Paul's
Epistles.*

Sunt hic duae universitates, Oxonia et Cantabrigia,
quarum utraque ambit habere me; nam Cantabrigiae
menses complures docui Graecas et sacras literas,
sed gratis, et ita facere semper decretum est. Sunt
130 hic collegia, in quibus tantum est religionis, tanta
vitae modestia, ut nullam religionem non sis prae
hac contempturus, si videas. Est Londini dominus
Ioannes Coletus, Divi Pauli Decanus, vir qui summam
doctrinam cum admirabili pietate copulavit, magnae
135 apud omnes auctoritatis. Is me sic amat, id quod
sciunt omnes, ut cum nemine vivat libentius quam
mecum; ut omittam alios innumeros, ne sim bis
molestus et iactantia et loquacitate.

Iam ut de operibus meis dicam aliquid, Adagiorum
140 opus ab Aldo impressum an videris nescio. Est
quidem profanum, sed ad omnem doctrinam util-
issimum; mihi certe inaestimabilibus constitit
laboribus ac vigiliis. Edidi opus De rerum verbor-
umque Copia, quod inscripsi Coleto meo, opus
145 utilitissimum contionaturis; at ista contemnunt ii

qui omnes bonas contemnunt literas. His duobus
annis praeter alia multa castigavi Divi Hieronymi
Epistolas; adulterina et subditicia obelis iugulavi,
obscura scholiis illustravi. Ex Graecorum et anti-
quorum codicum collatione castigavi totum Novum 150
Testamentum, et supra mille loca annotavi non sine
fructu theologorum. Commentarios in Epistolas
Pauli incepi, quos absolvam, ubi haec edidero.
Nam mihi decretum est in sacris immori literis.

*155–180. As to my dress, I adopted the Parisian fashion,
with the permission of the Bishop of Utrecht—a linen scapular
and a black hood. In Italy I wore a black robe and a
scapular, but in Bologna I was mistaken for a plague doctor,
and twice attacked by ruffians. I therefore concealed the
scapular, which was the cause of the misunderstanding, and
obtained leave from the Pope to discard the monastic habit if
I wished.*

Nunc restat ut de ornatu quoque tibi satisfaciam. 155
Semper antehac usus sum cultu canonicorum, et ab
Episcopo Traiectino, cum essem Lovanii, impetravi
ut sine scrupulo uterer scapulari lineo pro veste
linea integra, et capitio nigro pro pallio nigro, iuxta
morem Lutetiorum. Cum autem adirem Italiam 160
videremque toto itinere canonicos nigra veste uti
cum scapulari, ne quid offenderem novitate cultus,
veste nigra illic uti coepi cum scapulari. Postea
pestis orta est Bononiae, et illic qui curant peste
laborantes linteum album ex humero pendens ex 165
more gestant; hi congressus hominum fugitant.
Itaque cum die quodam doctum amicum viserem,
quidam nebulones eductis gladiis parabant me

invadere, et fecissent, ni matrona quaedam ad-
170 monuisset ecclesiasticum me esse. Altero item die
cum Thesaurarii filios adirem, undique cum fustibus
in me concurrerunt, et pessimis clamoribus adorti
sunt. Itaque a bonis viris admonitus occultavi
scapulare, et impetravi veniam a Pontifice Iulio
175 Secundo ut ornatu religionis uterer aut non uterer,
ut mihi visum esset, modo haberem vestem sacer-
dotalem; et si quid ante peccatum esset ea in re,
iis literis id totum condonavit. In Italia ergo per-
severavi in veste sacerdotali, ne mutatio esset alicui
180 scandalo.

181–194. *In England I found that the dress which I
proposed to adopt would not be acceptable. I put it away,
and availed myself of the Pope's dispensation. To return to
a monk's habit now would only cause offence.*

Postquam autem in Angliam redii, decrevi meo
solito uti ornatu, et domum accersito amico quodam
ostendi cultum quo uti statuissem. Rogavi an in
Anglia conveniret. Probavit, atque ita in publicum
185 prodii. Statim admonitus sum ab aliis amicis eum
cultum in Anglia ferri non posse, ut celarem potius.
Celavi; et quoniam non potest ita celari quin
aliquando deprehensus scandalum pariat, reposui in
scrinium et vetere summi Pontificis auctoritate sum
190 usus usque adhuc. Coactus deposui in Italia, ne
occiderer; deinde coactus deposui in Anglia, quia
tolerari non poterat, cum ipse multo maluerim uti.
At nunc denuo recipere plus gigneret scandali quam
mutatio ipsa gignebat.

195–214. Such are the principles on which I have based my life. I wish we could talk over the subject together; letters are very uncertain. Do not write anything confidential to me unless you are sure that the letter will reach me. I am on my way to Basel, and shall possibly be in Rome during the winter. I shall try to meet you some time on my return.

Habes universam vitae meae rationem, habes 195 meum consilium. Atque utinam liceat hisce de rebus coram inter nos commentari; nam literis nec satis commode nec satis tuto licet. Tuae enim quanquam per certissimos missae sic tamen aberrarant, ut nisi ipse casu me in arcem hanc contulissem, 200 nunquam fuerim visurus; et accepi iam a compluribus ante inspectas. Quare ne quid scripseris arcani, ni certo cognoveris ubi locorum sim et nuntium nactus sis fidissimum. Peto nunc Germaniam, id est Basileam, editurus lucubrationes meas, hac hieme 205 fortassis futurus Romae. In reditu dabo operam ut pariter colloquamur alicubi. Sed nunc aestas ferme praeteriit et longum est iter. Literas tuas tertio a Pascha die scriptas accepi Nonis Iuliis. Rogo ut salutem meam tuis piis votis Christo commendare ne 210 neglegas. Bene vale, quondam sodalis suavissime, nunc pater observande.

Ex arce Hammensi iuxta Calecium postridie Nonas Iulias Anno 1514.

NOTES

I

2. **Sonuerat diu tuba,** etc.: The fight is described in military metaphors in this and the following sentence. Erasmus is introducing as much 'vocabulary' as possible, for the benefit of his pupil.

4. **hic:** adverb, 'on this occasion.'

5. **haec:** sc. *acta sunt.*

6. **catastrophen:** acc. sing. of the Greek word 'catastrophe,' meaning the 'climax' of a drama.

7. **a pugna:** 'after the fight,' a common use of the preposition, cf. *a prandio,* after lunch.

concinnatura: fut. partic. implying 'purpose.'

8. **inter confabulandum:** *inter* = 'during,' is one of the few prepositions besides *ad* and *in* that are used with gerunds or gerundives.

9. **voce conviciisque:** abl. of respect, 'in voice, etc.'

10. **cesserit:** perf. subj. of virtual *oratio obliqua*; the clause gives the grounds on which he based his praise.

optasse me: indirect statement depending on a verb of saying implied in *laudo.* Latin slips easily into reported speech; it is better to supply an introducing verb in English.

quantum . . . tantundem: reverse the clauses in English: literally, 'just as strong with her hands also (*et*), as she was strong with her tongue.'

12. **vel:** a single *vel* is usually best translated 'even' or 'actually'; with a superlative adj., e.g. *vel optimus,* 'perhaps' will best render it; *vel . . . vel* is of course 'either . . . or.'

13. **pugnis:** from *pugnus,* not *pugna.*

14. **usque adeone . . . habes:** *lit.* 'Have you to such an extent . . .' Translate, 'Have you really . . . .'

15. **ista:** neut. pl., 'such treatment as that.'

19. **roganti:** sc. *ei.*

20. **caliendrum:** not exactly a wig, but false hair piled up on top of the head; it is classical Latin.

21. **mulierculae:** Erasmus is very fond of such diminutive formations, e.g. *corpusculum, domuncula*; the diminutive termination implies a variety of ideas, such as smallness, weakness, or sometimes affection. Here 'ladies' is perhaps adequate.

    mire sibi placent: 'are very proud of.'

24. **itidem accipi:** 'taken in the same spirit.'

26. **vulgato cognomine dictus:** 'commonly known as,' 'nicknamed.'

27. **Gerson:** a corruption of 'Garçon.'

31. **res ipsa:** 'the actual scene.'

33. **glomeribus:** *glomus* means literally 'a skein of wool'; here 'handfuls' might translate it.

37. **hoc est:** 'namely,' *i.e.*

39. **surdae cecinisse fabulam:** A proverbial expression; 'waste one's breath' or 'fall on deaf ears' might be used to translate it.

40. **venefica:** *lit.* 'a female poisoner.' It frequently meant 'witch,' which will do to translate it here.

44. **excusare:** 'plead by way of excuse.' Historic infinitive, as also *tractare*.

47. **dominae non subolere:** *subolet mihi* = lit. 'it smells to me,' *i.e.* 'I have a suspicion, inkling.' Shakespeare uses the same metaphor in *Twelfth Night*. 'Excellent! I smell a device,' says Sir Toby Belch, referring to Maria's scheme against Malvolio; to which Sir Andrew Aguecheek echoes, 'I have it in my nose too' (*mihi quoque subolet*).

2

1. **vir integerrime:** *integer* sometimes has the meaning 'honest.' Translate perhaps, 'Honoured Sir.'

3. **nomine tuo:** 'on your account.'

7. **quibus ei quibus opus erat:** the first *quibus* is abl. of time, 'during which'; the second is abl. of the thing needed, after the phrase *opus erat*.

8. **curatur:** 'looked after,' not 'cured'; though *curo* is occasionally used in the medical sense, it is not the usual meaning.

9. **ex me natus:** 'my own son.'

10. **mores . . . tolerabiles:** not a very flattering 'character report'; **pro ea aetate:** 'considering his youth.'

19. **patria:** *i.e.* the Netherlands.

22. **pro opera sua:** 'in return for his trouble.'

23. **quod de ratione diminutum erat:** 'the balance of the account,' the amount still owing.

29. **salute et vita:** ablatives of comparison; *antiquior* in the sense of 'more important' is a thoroughly classical use.

35. **habes de:** literally, 'you have (an account) of'; 'I have told you about.'

36. **animo:** 'intentions.'

38. **neque miseris:** the colloquial prohibition, 'do not send.'

43. **finis:** 'end' or 'goal.'

49. **pluribus:** sc. *verbis*, 'at greater length.'

50. **neque facile id potuissem:** A most revealing statement about the use of Latin in medieval times. Like all the leading scholars of Europe, Erasmus spoke, wrote, and probably thought almost entirely in Latin; his native Dutch had got a bit rusty. Though he spent much time in England, he never found it necessary to learn English properly, and one of his reasons for hestitating to accept the living of Aldington, in Kent, which Archbishop Warham offered him, was that he could not perform his duties as Rector owing to his inability to speak English.

51. **potuissem, intellexisses:** conditional subjunctives.

53. **ita tibi tuisque persuadeas:** 'you and your family may rest assured.'

3

2. **febri quotidiana:** a 'quotidian fever' is one that recurs every day, or night: **lenta** means 'obstinate' or 'persistent.'

6. **habe:** 'know.'

7. **obolere:** literally, 'smells'; here, 'grows stale.'

9. **uni Deo:** 'for God alone.'

11. **collegio:** the College of Montaigu, in Paris, where Erasmus studied.

12. **nihil:** translate 'no one'; *nihil* is regularly used in this sense.

vigilias, ieiunia: Erasmus is thinking here of his early life in a monastery, before he entered the service of the Bishop of Cambrai. In many letters he declares that his physical inability to endure the rigours of a monastic life was one of the main reasons for his abandoning it. He also found the living conditions in the College in Paris too much for his delicate constitution (see Introduction to Letter 1, and Letter 23).

20. **anno iubileo:** Year of Indulgence, granted by the Pope.

21. **istic:** literally, 'there where you are,' *i.e.* in the Netherlands. Bostius lived in Ghent.

vitam componere: 'settle down.'

23. **volumus, possimus:** Latin frequently uses the 1st pers. plur. for the 1st pers. sing., especially in correspondence. English never does this, but uses 'you' for both sing. and plur.

24. **veniri . . . vivi:** This impersonal passive construction is often difficult to render in English. The best way is generally to turn the verbs into nouns, and supply some suitable verb to complete the sense; *e.g.* 'the journey to Italy is very expensive.'

28. **prolixius . . . praestat:** 'his promises are always more generous than his performance.' The previous sentence can be turned in a similar way.

29. **Ipse . . . instem:** 'It is probably my own fault for not pressing him.' *Qui* with the subjunctive is here causal.

30. **vel:** 'even,' 'actually.'

31. **pro tempore:** 'according to circumstances.'

4

3. **et tamen labor:** 'and a hard task it was too.'

5. **dolor:** 'resentment,' 'annoyance.'

7. **agentem:** 'living'; the verb is frequently used in this sense either without an object, or in phrases like *tempus agere, vitam agere.*

animi causa: 'for recreation.'

11. **non solum . . . Montioiicae:** if fully expressed, the sentence would run: '*non solum (pompa) domūs illius, sed etiam (pompa domūs) Montioiicae.*'

13. **quandam, quadam**: Best omitted in translation. Latin tends to use *quidam* in order to soften a strong assertion, or to apologise for a metaphor, where no apology would be needed in English. Cicero, for example, wishing to emphasise that all liberal studies 'have a common bond and are closely related to one another,' says, '*habent quoddam commune vinculum et quasi cognatione quadam inter se continentur*' (*pro Archia*, 1, 2).

15. **a dextris**: 'on the right.'

18. **Nam**, etc.: The sentence begins with 'For' because it gives the reason why Edmond was not 'playing about' like Mary, or possibly why he was not present at all.

20. **rege**: in apposition to *quo*; 'under whom as king.'

23. **aliquo pacto**: = *aliquo modo*, 'somehow.'

25. **quod non praemonuisset**: The subjunctive is 'sub-oblique,' expressing the reason as present in Erasmus' mind. English can hardly make this subtle distinction without some clumsy periphrasis being inserted, such as 'as I thought to myself.' The same explanation will hardly account for *provocaret* being in the subjunctive; this is probably due to mere 'attraction.'

5

1. **priusquam ingrederer**: There seems no reason for the subjunctive here, unless Erasmus means to suggest that he could not set sail in time to prevent the loss of his money.

5. **cum**: 'although.'

7. **efferrem**: subjunctive in Oratio Obliqua.

9. **non esse fas**: see Introduction.

11. **tanti mihi constitit**: 'so much did it cost me.'

12. **ubi rediissem**: classical Latin would write an indicative after *ubi*.

18. **verterem animum**: 'alter my feelings.'

20. **privatum . . . regioni**: 'blame the country for a private misfortune.'

22. **vel in me vel in amicos**: to be taken after *provocarem iram*: 'rouse wrath against. . . .'

6

24. **testatum facerem**: Another purpose clause introduced by the *ut* at the beginning of the sentence; 'in
order to prove.' *Testatus* = 'evidence' or 'proof' is not a
classical word.

me nihilo secius . . . affectum: 'that my friendly
feelings towards him were just the same as they had been
before.'

26. **visum est**: 'it seemed good (to me),' 'I decided.'

28. **silvam**: a collection of selected passages, 'an
anthology.'

29. **hoc libelli**: the partitive genitive, a favourite construction with Erasmus, is rather pointless; the phrase means
no more than *hunc libellum*.

30. **versaturum . . . studiosorum** = 'would be read (or
used) by students.'

31. **quam non refrixissem**: The Indirect Question (like
quam non essem offensus below) is a substitute for an Indirect
Statement, and can only be translated as such.

6

2. **Adagia** is a plural word from *adagium*, 'a proverb';
hence the plural verbs in the next sentence.

ea sunt quae probari possint: 'it is the sort of book
which could win approval.'

4. **utile dulci,** etc.: An adaptation of the line of Horace
(*Ars Poetica*, 343): '*omne tulit punctum qui miscuit utile dulci*.'

5. **Tam iucundas . . . praecipio**: The order in translation is *non hortor modo, verum etiam . . . praecipio ut in
publicum proferas tam iucundas . . . lucubrationes*.

6. **lucubrationes**: literally, 'work done by lamplight,'
used by Cicero in the sense of 'a letter written at night.'
It is a favourite word with Erasmus and his correspondents, who use it simply with the meaning of 'literary
compositions.'

8. **ne videaris**: a purpose clause, not an indirect
command after *praecipio*.

9. **sudorem**: this metaphor for 'labours' is common in
classical Latin, but survives chiefly in schoolboy slang.

11. **subsannare:** A late Latin word meaning 'to insult by derisive gestures,' or 'mock at.'

non debent: 'Adagia' is the subject, an awkward change.

nasutum rhinocerota: The poet Martial has preserved the proverbial saying '*nasum rhinocerotis habere*,' meaning 'to turn up one's nose at everything.'

12. **sint allatura:** 'are likely to provide.'

14. **xv Iunii:** notice the modern style of date.

7

1. **quicquid . . . redibat:** 'all the income he derived.'

2. **quod erat patrimonii:** 'his private means.'

6. **servata:** The participle has a conditional force, 'if the money were hoarded.'

morbi: disease of the mind, not of the body: a vice or fault.

8. **opere magnifico:** ablative of description. Translate 'a splendid building.'

9. **in quibus agerent:** relative clause expressing purpose, 'for two schoolmasters to live in.'

10. **quo gratuito docerent:** *quo* for *ut* is generally reserved for purpose clauses containing a comparative adjective or adverb.

sic uti: 'with the limitation that.' The school was to contain 153 boys, the number of the miraculous draught of fishes.

12. **primus ingressus:** *lit.* 'the first entrance,' *i.e.* 'the first part, as you enter.'

13. **ceu catechumenos:** 'what I might call catechumens,' *i.e.* candidates under instruction for Confirmation; either 'New Boys' or 'the Preparatory School' would do.

nisi qui iam norit: 'unless he has already learnt how to.' *norit = noverit*.

15. **hypodidascalus:** 'Under Master,' a title still in use at St Paul's. Cicero in one of his letters borrows this word from the Greek.

16. **superior,** sc. *didascalus*: 'High Master,' still the proper title of the Head Master of St Paul's.

19. **docentis gestu**: 'in the attitude of one teaching.'

21. **Ipsum audite**: '(This is my Beloved Son,) hear ye Him.'

23. **rem divinam facere**: 'hold divine service.'

24. **secessus**: 'alcoves,' or 'rooms' opening off the main building.

29. **temere**: 'without consideration'; take *quosvis temere* together, and translate 'all and sundry.'

8

1. **de te nihil novi accepi**: 'I have heard no news about you,' *i.e.* about your prospects in England.

3. **eram his diebus**: 'I have been during the last few days.'

10. **eum qui habetur ex sapientioribus**: 'a man who is thought to be fairly sensible.'

11. **scholam**: St Paul's School, see Letter 7.

15. **poetae**: One can only translate this literally, putting 'poets' in inverted commas. Colet is referring to the more liberal, less hidebound education which his new School provided.

9

1. **dicimus salutem**: referring to the letters s.d. = *salutem dicit*, with which Latin letters generally begin. There is a play on the word *salutem*, which means either 'greeting' or 'health.'

5. **purgationis Mariae**: the Feast of the Purification of the Virgin Mary. Such a jest from an Archbishop is, to say the least of it, surprising.

quid sibi volunt: 'what is the meaning of.'

6. **super hanc petram**: a play on the words of Our Lord, 'Thou art Peter, and upon this Rock I will build my Church.'

7. **non construendo es**: 'it is not your intention to build.' This use of the dative of the gerund to express 'intention,' or 'ability,' is rare, but classical. The commonest expression is *solvendo esse* = 'to be in a position to pay,' *i.e.* 'to be solvent.'

9. **e re tua :** 'for your advantage,' 'any use to you.'

   cures, des : present subjunctive to express a command instead of the imperative.

11. **secus quam ego do pecuniam :** literally, 'otherwise' than I pay money.' Translate 'I, on the contrary, . . .'

15. **decem legiones :** meaning 'ten legions of angels,' referring to the words of Our Lord: 'I will ask the Father, and he will send me more than ten legions of angels.' There is a pun on the two senses of the word 'angel,' which is also the name of a coin.

15. **auri pharmacum :** gold was highly esteemed as a medicine in past ages. In the Prologue to the *Canterbury Tales*, Chaucer, with the same gentle humour as Warham, says of the Doctor of Physick,

> For gold in physick is a cordial (stimulant);
> Therefore he loved gold in special.

16. **energia :** 'efficacy,' a Greek word used in Late Latin.

20. **nec defraudes :** *nec* should be *neve*.

   aegritudine tua : ablative of cause; **spe, fructu,** ablatives depending on *defraudes*, 'deprive us of . . . .'

10

1. **Maecenas :** the friend of the Emperor Augustus, and the patron of Vergil.

   Abbatem : the Abbot of St Bertin, near St Omer, with whom Erasmus frequently stayed. Letter 13 was written at St Omer.

5. **nulli rerum successui fidendum esse :** 'one should never be confident that things will turn out well.'

9. **consternatur :** 'shied.'

11. **in diversum fertur :** 'jumped in the opposite direction.'

15. **explicandus :** literally, 'able to be expressed.' The gerundive frequently has this sense.

21. **longius erat iter quam ut confici posset :** 'the journey was too long to be accomplished.'

23. **quid fuerit animi :** 'what was my state of mind.'

divo Paulo: *divus,* properly applied to Roman Emperors deified after death, is used for 'Saint' in medieval Latin; *Divus Audumarus =* St Omer.

25. **hoc periculi:** Another instance of Erasmus' fondness for the partitive genitive; the phrase means little more than *hoc periculum;* cf. *hoc libelli* in Letter 5.

28. **ambulo lente:** it was the horse, of course, that walked, not Erasmus.

29. **fero:** 'I managed to endure it.'

31. **dolor se totum prodit:** literally, 'manifested itself entirely' (from *prodere,* not *prodire*).

a quiete: 'after rest.'

34. **me remisissem:** 'relaxed myself.'

35. **iacens . . . movere:** 'and if I lay down I could not make even the slightest movement.'

39. **procedit:** impersonal verb, 'the effort was successful.'

46. **ubicumque locorum ero:** 'wherever I am.' The phrase is similar to the more common *ubi gentium =* 'where on earth.'

II

3. **ubinam locorum es:** *cf.* Letter 10, line 46. The indicative moods of *es* and *vivis* in indirect questions cannot be justified. Erasmus usually avoids mistakes of this kind.

4. **votum Paulo, ut inquis, factum:** 'your vow made, as you say, to St Paul'; see the previous letter, line 23.

5. **tanti te factum fuisse:** 'that you were as highly honoured.' *Tanti* and *quanti* are genitives of value.

8. **Cantuariensis:** Archbishop Warham.

9. **Lincolniensis:** Thomas Wolsey: *regnat* suggests that he is the real ruler of the kingdom.

10. **Londiniensis:** see Introduction to Letter 8 for the relations between the Dean of St Paul's and his Bishop.

11. **Cartusienses:** not the Carthusian monastery near Smithfield Market, which in 1611 became Charterhouse School, but another at Richmond.

13. **mortuum mundo:** The literal translation 'dead to the world' had better be avoided!

14. **quo te conferes:** Another bit of bad Latin. What ought he to have written?

16. **xxᵉ die Octobr:** We have both methods of dating, the Roman and the modern, used in this letter. Notice that Erasmus' letter to Colet did not take an abnormally long time to get from Basel to London.

12

You will find this letter more difficult to translate adequately. It is formal, and consciously elaborate in style.

2. Conrad Peutunger came from Augsburg, and was, like Pirckheimer, an Imperial Councillor. He was one of the first serious archaeologists, and wrote a book on the Roman inscriptions in Germany.

amicitiae . . . conciliaturum esse: in simple language this means 'we became friends,' but as Willibald's language is rather flowery, we had better say something like 'you were united to me in the bonds of friendship.'

3. **operam:** 'kind office' or 'service.'

7. **quem unum,** etc.: English will get the emphasis by beginning 'he is the one notable man of all those unknown to me, whom I should most desire . . .'

11. **reliqua . . . videar:** 'I think I am pretty influential with the rest of the company of my friends.' *Belle* is a word that has much weakened in meaning, like the corresponding English words 'pretty' (as an adverb) and 'fairly.' 'Fairly' has gone even further downhill than 'pretty,' so that 'Industry fairly satisfactory' is not considered a good Report.

13. **non in ultimis bonis collocarem:** 'I should rank the friendship . . . among by no means the least of my possessions.'

16. **acquirere valeam:** 'succeed in gaining.'

18. **adduceres, prosequerer:** The regular tense for a condition or wish referring to the future is the present subjunctive.

21. **priusquam detur:** impersonal, 'until it is granted to me.'

¹³

2. **nobis:** = *mihi.*

3. **Novum Testamentum:** The great work of Erasmus'
life was his edition of the New Testament in the original
Greek, together with a Latin translation of his own, more
accurate than the Vulgate. This was begun during his
visit to England, 1509–14, while he was living in Queens'
College, Cambridge, and finally printed in Basel by John
Froben. It is not a work of great critical scholarship,
since he only used two Greek manuscripts lent to him by
Colet from the library of St Paul's, and a few inferior ones
which he found at Basel. But he had pointed the way,
and after him no scholar of the New Testament could be
content with anything but the Greek.

6. **fuit in causa quominus:** 'was the reason why I did
not . . .'

7. **Ghisberto:** Ghisbert was a doctor at St Omer,
who was closely connected with the Abbey of St Bertin,
where Erasmus frequently stayed.

puer: ' my servant.'

¹⁴

1. **Quas literas accepimus, nunc misimus:** 'I am now
sending you the literature which . . . .'

2. **Breve Leonis Pont.:** 'The Brief of Pope Leo.' A
Brief is a letter from the Pope, less formal than a Papal
Bull. The title *Pontifex* is a survival from early times, when
the Chief Priest of Rome was called Pontifex Maximus.

3. **Commendationis:** 'Letter of Recommendation.'

4. **Reuchlini:** see note to line 6 of Letter 16 for information about Reuchlin.

Picheymeri: Froben's spelling of Pirckheimer, the
writer of Letter 12.

6. **de Principis Institutione:** *The Education of a Prince,*
written by Erasmus for the Archduke Charles, afterwards
the Emperor Charles V.

7. **Hieronymus:** *i.e.* Erasmus' edition of the works of
St Jerome, one of the early Christian Fathers.

9. **Lotharingiae aditus:** 'the route to Lorraine.'

clausus esset: there is no reason for 'quod' to take a subjunctive.

13. **arriserit:** 'is satisfactory'; literally, 'smiles upon us.'

14. **describebatur:** 'copied out' in manuscript.

15. **tum in medio tum in calce:** 'not only in the middle, but also at the end.' *tum . . . tum* is a later variety of the classical *cum . . . tum*. '*calce*': there are two words *calx* in Latin; one means 'heel,' the other 'limestone' or 'chalk.' This second word then came to mean 'end of a race-track,' because it was marked by a chalk-line; finally, in later Latin, it could be used for the end of a page or book.

19. **Moriam:** *The Praise of Folly*, perhaps Erasmus' best-known book (see Introduction, p. 5).

24. **sodalitas:** the 'company' includes the printing-works staff, as well as Froben's family.

26. **calcographus:** 'printer.'

15

1. **Kalendis Maii:** *Maius* is here used as a noun meaning the month of May; the classical form would be *Kalendis Maiis—Maius* being used as an adjective.

2. **scaphula nautica eiecti sumus:** 'we were landed from a ship's boat.'

4. **quos litus vicinum nobis exasperavit:** literally, 'which the near-by shore made harsh for us.' Some paraphrase is necessary.

5. **Ii:** sc. *venti*.

6. **cynanche, pleuritide:** Greek medical terms already latinised in classical times; Roman medicine relied entirely on the Greeks. The old form of 'quinsy' was 'squinancy,' showing its derivation from 'cynanche.'

9. **incidit incommode quod reversus offenderim:** 'unfortunately, when I returned, I found Peter, etc.' *accidit* or *incidit quod* is a fairly common substitute for *accidit ut*, but Erasmus need not have used the subjunctive.

11. **nec citra periculum:** literally, 'and not on this side of danger,' *i.e.* 'dangerously ill.' This is an expressive,

though not classical use of the preposition, which is a favourite with Erasmus; *cf.* Letter 15, line 153. *citra syncopim* = 'short of fainting.'

12. **belle valebamus:** for *belle* see note on Letter 12, line 12.

14. **purgandae bili:** dative expressing 'purpose.'

16. **a pharmaco sumpto:** 'after taking the medicine.'

20. **equo:** there are many references in Erasmus' correspondence to this English horse; it is presumably the *Anglus equus* which let him down so badly during the journey described in Letter 18.

16

1. **quantum . . . tantum:** These 'proportion' sentences are always difficult to translate literally. You can say 'my distress at hearing . . . is equalled by my joy,' or 'distressed as I am to hear . . ., I am equally glad . . .' Fisher is referring to the voyage mentioned in the previous letter.

6. **quo . . . donatum:** literally, 'with which you write that I have been presented by Reuchlin.' Reuchlin was a distinguished scholar, who was among the first to introduce into Germany the study of Hebrew and Greek. He was violently attacked by the monks and friars, and actually handed over to the Inquisition as a heretic. Erasmus wrote letters to Rome in his defence, in which he lashes with invective the converted Jew, named Pfeffercorn, who was Reuchlin's chief opponent, calling him 'a child of hell disguised as an angel of light.' The excitements of the Reformation caused Reuchlin's case to be forgotten, and he was released from prison.

10. **tuae in me humanitatis studia:** 'proofs of your anxiety to show kindness to me.' The plural of abstract words generally implies 'instances of' the quality or feeling mentioned; e.g. *irae* means 'outbursts of anger.'

14. **me gratias . . . habere maximas:** 'that my gratitude to him is as great as I can possibly conceive.'

16. **Testamento Novo:** see Letter 13, line 3. This sentence is a fine appreciation of its value by one of the most saintly and learned of Englishmen. *quando*, 'since,' *ut*, consecutive.

25. **illum:** the printer.

26. **Tibi et istud debeo, quod . . . possum:** 'To you I also owe this, that I can . . .' Erasmus had helped the Bishop with his Greek; this explains why Fisher signs himself 'discipulus tuus.'

28. **respondeant:** 'agree with.'

17

1. **Hispaniarum Rex:** Charles V, Emperor, 1519.

10. **mea sors solius:** 'my fate alone': *solius* is genitive agreeing with *mei* understood.

11. **purpurati:** 'high officials of Court.' The word is used by Cicero.

13. **illa insula:** the Isle of Walcheren.

14. **ea est:** 'such is.'

22. **vestrates Hollandicas:** 'peat from your native Holland.' Like *vestras* and *nostras*, and *cuias?* = 'of what country?' **thus olere** = 'smell of incense.'

27. **ne . . . divertas fossarum altitudo vetat:** What is the usual construction after *vetare?*

29. **arcendo mari:** dative of the gerundive, expressing purpose.

31. **sexcentas:** used in Latin to express any large number, like our 'thousand.' It may have been chosen because the Roman cohort originally consisted of 600 men.

quibus linum macerant: 'in which they soak the flax.' The first process in the preparation of flax for manufacture into linen is the rotting down of the stalks, variously known as 'retting,' 'chapelling,' or 'steepling.'

33. **putent:** does not come from *putare*.

35. **reditus:** a noun, subject of the sentence.

43. **herbam porrigere:** 'throw up the sponge.' It is said that in primitive Roman times, at rustic sports, the loser admitted his defeat by plucking some grass and handing it to his opponent.

45. **tacitis:** Supply *eis rebus* to complete the abl. abs., and as the antecedent to the relative clause. Literally, 'those things not being mentioned which, etc.' *Taceo* can

be used as a transitive verb meaning 'to pass over in silence'; hence it can have a past participle passive meaning 'unmentioned.' Compare *reticebo* in line 49.

51. **ut**: 'according as . . .'

57. **priusquam obsignarem**: 'before I had time to seal.' The subjunctive implies 'something prevented.'

18

3. **ut qui . . . gratiam**: a causal clause, 'as I had not yet become reconciled to the open air.'

5. **idque**: 'and that too'; *id* sums up the previous clause; *cf.* line 17.

9. **plus semihoram**: *quam* is omitted after *plus* and *amplius*; *cf.* line 16, *plus sexaginta*.

illi: *i.e.* the innkeeper and his staff; *cf.* line 20, *illorum*.

13. **merae nauseae**: 'absolutely revolting!'

16. **hypocausto**: here means a basement room, probably heated by a stove. Originally the word means the sweating room in a Roman bath, heated from beneath by hot air, which was also carried up the walls through hollow tiles.

17. **ad horam decimam**: Erasmus is here using the modern, not the Roman method of reckoning, *cf.* line 24.

19. **ad illorum clepsydras**: 'until their clocks showed the time for dinner.' In Roman times the *clepsydra*, water-clock, was used to measure the length of speeches in the Senate, just as later, an hourglass timed the sermon in the pulpit. Mechanical clocks had been invented in Erasmus, day, but were not common. An inn would probably use either an hourglass or a water-clock.

21. **multa adhuc nocte**: 'while it was still dark.'

23. **prandium**: This is the French *déjeuner*, lunch. As in Roman days, it was the first main meal of the day.

25. **Schurerio**: Schurer was a member of a distinguished Literary Society at Strasbourg. On his way through the city, four years before, Erasmus had been welcomed with great enthusiasm by the Society, which made him an honorary member.

27. **cum:** 'although.'

31. **Maternum meum vicinum:** 'my friend Maternus, who lived next door.'

34. **forte fortuna:** stronger than *forte*; 'by good luck.'

37. **Caesaris:** the Emperor.

41. **navigatio . . . studio: nautarum studio** should be taken with the first clause; **nisi . . . erat** is a parenthesis.

47. **Cinicampius:** a good example of the slightly affected practice among scholars of latinising names; Eschenfelder = Ash-field. Sometimes names were turned into Greek, *e.g.* Schwarzerde (black earth) becomes Melanchthon.

48. **incredibile dictu quam . . . :** literally, 'it is unbelievable to say how . . .'

49. **syngraphas telonicas:** 'customs accounts.'

53. **alteros:** 'two more.'

55. **qui . . . advexerint:** relative clause with the subjunctive, expressing cause, 'because they had brought to him.'

officii gratia: 'as a mark of respect.'

56. **dominus:** a clerical title, 'Master John'; *cf.* the name of the Priest in *Twelfth Night*, Sir John Topaz.

61. **moribus compositis:** 'of mature character.'

62. **iureconsultissimus:** 'an expert lawyer.'

70. **mando de . . . :** 'I entrusted the task of . . .'

71. **ad decimam:** 'by ten o'clock.'

72. **de biga non successit:** the verb is impersonal, as in line 74; 'no luck about the carriage.'

74. **Sensi . . . haererem:** 'I realised the situation. It was a plot to keep me there.' What does it mean literally?

78. **Comitem Novae Aquilae:** 'The Count of Neuenahr,' German for New Eagle.

80. This is a quotation from Horace.

85. **successit:** not impersonal, as in lines 72, 74.

86. **vento suo:** 'The wind which brought it.'

87. **quae:** the antecedent is **quassationem.**

91. **convivium agitabant:** The Cathedral clergy, canons, precentor, vice-provost, etc., took it in turns to supply the meals (*cf.* line 100).

103. **a baculo quo contunditur:** 'from the stick with which it is beaten'; dried fish needs the same treatment as beefsteak to make it tender.

113. **sorbitiuncula**: 'a posset,' a drink of hot spiced ale or wine, apparently Erasmus' favourite remedy for a chill on the stomach.

120. **magis conveniret**: 'it would have been more suitable.'

121. **non parum habet rusticitatis**: literally, 'has not too little rusticity.' Translate, 'is extremely primitive.'

124. **quo magis libebat**: 'so I was the more anxious.'

142. **mihi visum est**: 'I thought it better.'

147. **vel manu contacta**: 'with a mere touch.'

151. **divi Trudonis**: the town of St Trond.

153. **caelo vespertino offensus**: 'when exposed to the evening air.'

157. **quam graviter tulerit Episcopus**: 'how annoyed the Bishop was.'

160. **quae Lovanium peteret**: A good example of the 'generic' subjunctive. This was 'the coach going to Louvain,' the Louvain coach; *quae L. petebat* would mean 'a coach which was going to L.'

19

This will be much easier 'to translate if Letter 18 has already been done, because many people and incidents in that letter are referred to.

6. **mihi satis placerem**: 'I was very pleased with myself.'

9. **antiqua nobilitate**: 'old - fashioned nobility of character.'

11. **non una in disciplina**: 'in more than one branch of learning.'

13. **militibus**: The Count was a soldier.

14. **Bobardiae**: Erasmus spells this place 'Popardia' in Letter 18.

21. **sycophantas agunt**: 'play the part of sycophants.' *agere* is used in a theatrical sense.

22. **ut ad rem**: sc. *redeam*, 'to return to my story.'

23. **laetus laetos**: Translate, 'to our mutual delight.'

28. **tria ulcera**: Boils were one of the signs of plague, but Erasmus in another letter accounts for one of these

three, by saying that it was caused by his servant rubbing his back too hard with rose-oil, as a cure for a pain in his kidneys.

32. **mihi cum chirurgis res est:** 'I have been in the surgeons' hands.' Notice the Latin use of the present tense, to describe something which lasts up to the time of speaking.

36. **suffecturum fuisse:** 'would have survived.'

37. **Christus Opt. Max.:** This title is taken over by Christianity from the Roman religion: *Iuppiter Optimus Maximus*. **his:** abl. of comparison.

39. **modo non sinat:** 'provided that he does not allow.' Classical Latin would write *modo ne*, or *dum ne*.

20

4. **D.** = *Dominus*, 'Master.'

5. **quod credas:** The subjunctive can be explained as emphasising that the reason is Sir Henry Guildford's own, and that Erasmus takes no responsibility for the truth of it. *Quod faveas* in line 7 is similar.

9. **non quod . . . persuasum est:** The 'rejected reason' takes the subjunctive *praeditus sim*; the real reason which follows takes the indicative *persuasum est*.

11. **ad pietatem faciunt:** 'make for, conduce to piety.'

22. **illis vacantibus:** 'while they devote themselves to.'

40. This sentence provides many examples of the gerundive used instead of the gerund, to translate the English verbal noun.

46. **quo:** ablative after *frui*.

47. **quippe qui accedam:** 'since I am approaching.'

49. **officiorum:** 'services.'

53. **hoc maiorem habeo gratiam, quod . . .:** 'I am the more grateful, because . . .'

56. **istum animum tibi, te nobis servet:** 'may he keep that spirit in you, and preserve you for me.' 'That spirit' means 'those feelings of affection and kindness.'

57. **Opt. Max.:** see Letter 19, line 37.

58. **studio certe nulli cessurum:** 'one who will certainly not take second place to anyone in devotion to you.'

21

1. **qui:** 'how.'

7. **possit:** potential subjunctive 'could be.'

9. **nihil habent pensi:** 'have no consideration for,' 'do not consider.' *pensi*, partitive genitive of *pensum*, 'weight, or importance.'

11. **Galenus:** The two great physicians of antiquity, upon whose work medieval medicine was based, were Hippocrates (400 B.C.) and Galen, who lived at Rome in the second century A.D.

14. **colatam:** literally 'filtered.' The kitchen utensil 'colander' comes from the verb *colare*; *aura colata* = 'draught.'

15. **quiescentem:** 'because it remains stagnant.'

23. **adde quod:** literally, 'add the fact that'; 'furthermore.'

25. **ne quid dicam:** 'not to mention.'

26. **salsamentis:** A good deal of the leprosy, which was very prevalent in England, was probably due to the excessive consumption of salted meat and fish. Gilbert White, in the *Natural History of Selborne*, written in the second half of the eighteenth century, is of this opinion. 'Some centuries ago,' he writes, 'this horrible distemper prevailed all Europe over. It must therefore be, to a humane and thinking person, a matter of equal wonder and satisfaction when he contemplates how nearly this pest is eradicated, and observes that a leper now is a rare sight. This happy change may have originated from the much smaller quantity of salted meat and fish now eaten in these kingdoms'; and he goes on to explain how improved methods of agriculture have so altered the situation that 'no man needs eat salted flesh, unless he prefers it, that has money to buy fresh.'

27. **confiderem:** literally, 'I should be confident.' Translate, 'I am quite sure.'

28. **tolleretur:** 'were abolished.'

31. **et:** 'even.'

36. **si fueram ingressus:** 'if ever I entered.'

38. **conferret huc:** 'it would be an additional advantage'; literally, 'it would contribute to this.'

si vulgo . . . posset: 'if the people could be persuaded to adopt . . .' Notice that *persuadeo* is used here as a transitive verb; literally, 'if a more sparing diet could be persuaded to the people'; *cf.* line 49.

40. **aedilibus:** 'town magistrates.' In addition to looking after the corn supply of Rome, and providing public amusements such as gladiatorial shows, the Roman *aediles* were responsible for keeping the streets clean and controlling the water-supply.

41. **curarentur et ea . . . essent:** '(and if) the outskirts of the city were also looked after.'

43. **qui sollicitus sim:** a causal clause, 'since I am anxious.'

46. **quin tu . . . noris:** 'that you in your wisdom know better about these things.' *noris = noveris*, perf. subj. *novi* = I know (perf. of *nosco*).

22

1. **multa nova:** There was an old proverb, 'Africa always produces something new.' Erasmus' Africa here is the city of Basel, where religious changes, which he does not favour, were just being introduced.

6. **hortum, quem satis amplum:** 'the fairly large garden, which . . .' Notice the Latin idiom by which emphatic adjectives and superlatives are placed inside the relative clause: *e.g.* 'the best slave he had' = *servus, quem optimum habebat*.

13. **Chrysostomo:** St Chrysostom was one of the Christian Fathers. Erasmus spent much of his life in translating and editing their works.

14. **fulmen:** usually translated 'thunderbolt,' but here must mean 'thunder flash,' since it is described as *tacitum*.

16. **prospicio si se vertisset caelum:** 'I looked out to see if the weather had changed.' *Si* is not a mistake for *num* in an indirect question, but means 'in case.'

21. **cuius modi . . . solet:** 'almost the same sort of noise as is generally heard.'

27. **sese proferentis in sublime:** 'rising up on high.' The participle agrees with *nubis*.

7

29. **dixisses:** conditional subjunctive with the 'if' clause suppressed: 'you would have said' (if you had seen it).

30. **quo attentius . . . hoc minus:** 'The more closely . . . the less . . .'

35. **sicubi fuerit exortum incendium:** 'if a fire breaks out anywhere.'

41. **multis obviis armatis:** 'meeting many armed men.'

45. **cum:** 'although.'

47. **nescioquorum incuria:** 'through some people's carelessness.'

48. **quod si . . . fuisset:** 'now if this quantity of powder had been at the top.'

    modo: 'only.'

50. **attigit:** 'touched off.'

52. **impetus incendii . . . ferendo:** 'the force of the fire tried to find out whether it could stand the weight.' *oneri ferendo* is called a 'dative of purpose,' as in the phrase *solvendo esse* = 'to be solvent, able to pay.'

54. **idque testantur qui viderunt:** 'and to this fact those people bear witness who saw . . .'

60. **aliam alio sparsit:** 'scattered them (the four parts) in different directions.'

63. **vidisses:** cf. *dixisses,* line 29.

65. **deferri, demoliri:** infinitives depending on *vidisses.*

66. **longo tractu:** 'over a wide area.'

67. **curarat aediculas quasdam exstruendas:** 'had had some small houses built.'

72. **quod vulgo dici solet:** 'the common saying.' The clause is the subject of *putabatur.*

23

3. **Angliam egressum:** Erasmus had spent four years in England, his longest and probably his last visit, though he may have made a short stay in 1516. Servatius' letter had been sent off three months before (see line 208), *egredior* is here a transitive verb.

6. **utpote ex itinere scribens:** *utpote* adds the notion of 'cause' to the participle; 'since I am writing.' The journey was to Basel.

9. **non quod probarem:** subjunctive of 'rejected reason.'

The real reason is contained in the purpose clause which follows.

10. **scandalo :** predicative dative.

11. **tutorum pertinacia :** see Introduction for the story of how Erasmus was forced by his guardians into the monastery of Steyn. Cornelius of Woerden was an old acquaintance who had become a monk, and helped the guardians to break down Erasmus' resistance.

14. **cum :** 'although.'

17. **corporis ratione :** 'constitution.'

20. **quarum illic nullus usus :** This does not necessarily imply that learning was unknown at Steyn, because Erasmus managed to read a great deal of the classics there; he means that a monastery is not the right place for a scholar. 'Where there is no scope for it' would perhaps get the meaning best.

21. **obiciet annum :** 'taunt me with the year.' *obicere* is to bring up something against a person.

24. **norit** = *noverit*, from *nosco*.

30. **multis vitiis :** Erasmus was not blind to his own weaknesses : he admits in line 38 that he was prone to indulgence in pleasures.

31. **consuetudinem habere cum :** 'enjoy the society of.'

viri vere Christum sapientibus : 'men of truly Christian character.' *sapere* originally meant 'to have the flavour of,' 'to taste of.'

40. **contubernio :** literally, 'tent-companionship.' In the Roman army it meant 'a number of soldiers living together in one tent,' a 'mess.' Hence it comes to mean 'a society.'

succurrebat : 'occurred to me,' 'came into my mind.'

42. **frigida :** 'dull.'

43. **cui :** 'from which.' Verbs which signify 'taking away,' such as *adimo, eripio*, are followed by the dative of the person from whom something is removed.

44. **expetendum :** gerundive, 'what you leave to be desired.'

46. **aetate et morbis et laboribus :** When Erasmus wrote this he was forty-eight, a ripe age in medieval times. Moralising on the illness from which he suffered in consequence of his journey from Basel to Louvain (Letter 18), he says, 'I have passed my fiftieth year, and since so few

reach this age, I cannot complain that I have not lived long enough.' In spite of his delicate health, he lived to be seventy. As for his '*labores*,' few men have toiled so incessantly, and his output was prodigious. His correspondence alone fills eight large volumes, and the books mentioned in this letter are only a small fraction of his works.

quae facit ut: 'the result of this is that.'

48. **calculo:** stone in the bladder. In Letter 9, Archbishop Warham hopes that Erasmus has recovered from an attack of the 'stone,' and makes some unclerical jokes on the subject.

49. **malo:** a noun, 'malady.'

50. **nihil bibo:** 'I have drunk nothing.' The present tense is correctly used of an action still going on at the time of speaking. Similarly, *nihil bibebam* means 'I had been drinking nothing.'

56. **nisi quod . . . attulissem:** 'except that I should have brought.'

59. **imponit ista persuasio:** 'that argument of yours deceives.'

61. **cultus:** 'dress.'

victus: 'food,' 'diet,' or perhaps 'way of life.'

caerimoniolis: the diminutive ending implies contempt; 'unimportant, petty ceremonies.'

62. **actum (esse) de illo:** 'that it is all up with . . .'

63. **commutarit, verterit, mutet:** consecutive or generic subjunctives, 'the sort of man who changes . . .' The first two are perf. subj. as referring to single, completed actions, while *mutet* is present, 'one who is always changing.'

65. **ausim:** an old form of the perfect subj. 'I should venture to say.'

66. **istis quas vocant religionibus:** 'your so-called religious practices.'

70. **Solonis:** Solon, the Athenian lawgiver of the sixth century B.C., departed from Athens for ten years, to give his laws a chance to prove themselves in practice. He made his fellow-citizens swear an oath to keep them during his absence.

Pythagoras: A native of Samos, he was one of the greatest of the early Greek philosophers (sixth century B.C.).

He travelled in Egypt and the East in search of knowledge, and died in South Italy.

71. **Plato:** After the death of his master Socrates, in 399 B.C., he left Athens and spent some time in Egypt, Italy and Sicily.

72. **Divus Hieronymus:** St Jerome, who died in A.D. 420, was one of the Latin Fathers of the Christian Church. Erasmus wrote an edition of his works (see line 147).

83. **quae non invitet:** consecutive subj. as in line 63.

87. **cum:** 'when,' 'since,' or 'although'?

88. **Cardinalis Grimanus:** Grimani was one of the most powerful Cardinals at this time; he lived in Venice, and possessed a famous library, which he bequeathed to a monastery there. It later passed into the possession of the Library of St Mark. Erasmus visited the Cardinal during his stay in Italy in 1509.

hic ipse: Pope Leo X, who succeeded the warlike Julius II in 1513. It was he who, in order to help to pay for the building of St Peter's at Rome, started the great sale of indulgences which moved Luther to fix his famous '95 theses' to the door of Wittenberg Church, and thus begin the Reformation. Leo was a great supporter of the New Learning, and approved of Erasmus' work on the New Testament. Erasmus dedicated to him his edition of *St Jerome.*

89. **ut ne dicam:** 'not to mention.'

96. **qui nolit domesticum:** 'who does not desire me as a guest in his house.'

98. **suapte:** emphatic form of *sua.*

99. **sic de me . . . amantius:** This must be paraphrased 'speaks of me with the utmost respect and affection.' What is the literal translation?

104. **eleemosynario:** The Royal Almoner at this time was Cardinal Wolsey, then Bishop of Lincoln. His duties are indicated in this sentence.

105. **Regina:** Catherine of Aragon.

106. **me:** subject of *accumulaturum.*

107. **quantum libeat sacerdotiorum:** 'as many livings as I like.'

114. **sacerdotium:** Archbishop Warham gave Erasmus the living of Aldington in Kent, but allowed him to resign

it, and take part of the stipend, paying the rest to a curate, who fulfilled the duties for him. 100 nobles = £33, 6s. 8d.; 100 crowns = £20.

118. **petenti**: sc. *mihi*.

121. **Dominus Montioius**: see Introduction, and letters 4, 5, 10.

125. **multa promittunt**: Erasmus had conceived high hopes of Henry's good intentions towards him. But the king was at this time occupied with preparations for war with France. Erasmus' disappointment was the main reason for his leaving England in 1514.

126. **Cantabrigia**: from 1510–13 Erasmus lived in Queens' College; he gave lectures in Greek, though he does not seem to have held any regular appointment. He taught Divinity also, as Lady Margaret Reader. In 1513 the plague drove him and most of the undergraduates away for some months.

131. **ut nullam religionem . . . contempturus**: 'that there is no religion which you would not despise compared with this.'

133. **Coletus**: Erasmus made his acquaintance during his first visit to England in 1499. It was he who encouraged Erasmus to publish the New Testament in the original Greek, though Colet himself only began to learn Greek later. See Letter 7 for an account of the founding of St Paul's School by Colet in 1510.

139. **Adagiorum opus**: For the *Adagia*, and how it came to be written, see Introduction to Letter 5. Aldus was a famous Venetian printer; Erasmus visited him in 1508, in order to see the second edition of the *Adagia* through the press. The Aldine Press was a meeting-place for many famous scholars.

142. **mihi constitit . . . laboribus**: *constare*, to cost, takes the dative of the person, and the ablative of the price.

143. **de Copia**: A treatise on Latin Composition, which supplied the beginner with many useful words and phrases. Dedicated to Colet, it was doubtless used by the scholars of St Paul's, as well as by preachers (*contionaturi*).

147. **castigavi**: 'I have produced a critical edition of.'

148. **adulterina . . . iugulavi**: 'I have marked with critical marks (††) corrupt and spurious passages.'

155. **de ornatu:** This is a rather complicated question, but perhaps the following explanation will make it clearer. Erasmus was an Augustinian Canon, whose proper dress consisted of a white cassock covered by a black cloak and hood. The Bishop of Utrecht allowed Erasmus to modify this by substituting a black hat, called a biretta, for the black cloak and hood, and a white linen scapular for the white cassock. A scapular is a short sleeveless cloak.

While he was at Bologna, in Italy, there was an outbreak of plague, and his white scapular caused him to be mistaken for one of the plague doctors, who wore a kind of white linen scarf as a distinguishing mark. Erasmus therefore thought it wise to conceal his scapular, and gained permission from Pope Julius to dispense with his monk's habit, as he thought fit, and wear the dress of an ordinary secular priest.

What happened in England is by no means clear. Erasmus intended to resume his modified monk's habit, but was warned that this would not be tolerated (why this should be, is not explained); he therefore availed himself of the Pope's dispensation and, as in Italy, appeared in the garb of an ordinary priest. It is hard to tell from his portraits what he is wearing, because he is wrapped up in heavy fur robes to keep out the cold, to which he was abnormally sensitive.

162. **ne quid offenderem:** 'so as not to give offence in any way.'

166. **ex more gestant:** 'are accustomed to wear.'

171. **Thesaurarii filios:** The sons of Archduke Philip's Treasurer, who were staying in Bologna, and later became firm friends with Erasmus.

179. **alicui scandalo:** 'a stumbling-block to anyone.'

186. **ut celarem potius:** *admonitus sum* takes two constructions, an indirect statement, followed by an indirect command; 'warned me that . . ., and advised me to . . .'

187. **non potest . . . pariat:** 'it cannot be so concealed as not to cause offence by being occasionally detected.'

200. **arcem:** Hammes Castle, see Introduction to this letter.

201. **nunquam fuerim visurus:** 'I should never have seen it.' This periphrastic construction is used when the main clause of a conditional sentence is also a Result clause.

202. This is a slightly irregular Conditional sentence. The main clause is a Prohibition, expressed by *ne* + Perfect Subjunctive; the Subordinate clause should regularly be in the Future Perfect, but *nactus sis* proves that both verbs are to be taken as Perfect Subjunctives. The normal English tense will be Present Indicative.

208. **tertio a Pascha die:** 'two days after Easter.' Why not 'three'?

213. **postridie Nonas:** What would be the classical form of this date?

INDEX OF PROPER NAMES

VOCABULARY

The following quantities only are marked:

(i) The Present Infinitive of Verbs of the Second Conjugation,
e.g. *habeo, -ēre.*

(ii) The Genitive Singular of Nouns of the Fourth Declension,
e.g. *status, -ūs.*

(iii) The Present Infinitive of Verbs of Mixed Conjugation,
e.g. *capio, -ĕre.*

(iv) A few words of similar form are distinguished, e.g. *ĕdo*
and *ēdo.*

See page 141 for additional words.

a, ab (*prep.* with *abl.*) : by,
from, after.

abbas, -atis (*m.*) : abbot.

abeo, -ire, -ivi or -ii, -itum (*v.i.*) :
go away, depart.

aberro, -are, -avi, -atum (*v.i.*) :
go astray.

abhorreo, -ēre, -ui (*v.i.*) : shrink
from.

absolvo, -ere, -i, -solutum (*v.t.*) :
finish off.

absque (*prep.* with *abl.*) : without.

absum, -esse, -fui (*v.i.*) : be
absent, distant.

ac : and, as.

accedo, -ere, -cessi, -cessum
(*v.t.* and *i.*) : approach, be
added.

accerso, -ere, -ivi, -itum (*v.t.*) =
arcesso : summon, send for.

accido, -ere, -i (*v.i.*) : happen.

accipio, -ĕre, -cepi, -ceptum
(*v.t.*) : receive, welcome, listen
to.

accumbo, -ere, -cubui, -cubitum
(*v.i.*) : sit down (to a meal).

accumulo, -are, -avi, -atum
(*v.t.*) : heap up.

accurro, -ere, -curri, -cursum
(*v.i.*) : run up.

acquiro, -ere, -quisivi, -quisitum
(*v.t.*) : obtain, win.

acuo, -ere, -ui, -utum (*v.t.*) :
sharpen.

ad (*prep.* with *acc.*) : to, towards,
near, about, for the purpose
of.

addo, -ere, -didi, -ditum (*v.t.*) :
add.

adduco, -ere, -duxi, -ductum
(*v.t.*) : bring, draw to (a
curtain).

adeo, -ire, -ivi or -ii, -itum
(*v.i.* or *t.*) : approach.

adhibeo, -ēre, -ui, -itum (*v.t.*) :
employ, show.

adhuc (*adv.*) : up to now,
still.

adicio, -ĕre, -ieci, -iectum
(*v.t.*) : add.

adigo, -ere, -egi, -actum (*v.t.*) :
drive, compel.

aditus, -ūs (*m.*) : approach.

adiungo, -ere, -iunxi, -iunctum
(*v.t.*) : connect, add.

admiror, -ari, -atus (*v.t.*) : be
astonished at, marvel at.

admitto, -ere, -misi, -missum (*v.t.*) : admit, let in.

admodum (*adv.*) : quite, very.

admoneo, -ēre, -ui, -itum (*v.t.*) : advise, recommend.

adorior, -iri, -ortus (*v.t.*) : attack, assail.

adorno, -are, -avi, -atum (*v.t.*) : decorate, saddle (a horse), equip, fit out, make ready.

adoro, -are, -avi, -atum (*v.t.*) : worship.

adrepo, -ere, -repsi, -reptum (*v.i.*) : creep, crawl.

adscisco, -ere, -scivi, -scitum (*v.t.*) : admit, attach.

adsum, -esse, -fui (*v.i.*) : be present.

adulterinus, -a, -um : corrupt.

adveho, -ere, -vexi, -vectum (*v.t.*) : carry.

adversus (*prep.* with *acc.*) : against.

advoco, -are, -avi, -atum (*v.t.*) : call, summon.

aedes, -ium (*f. pl.*) : house.

aedicula, -ae (*f.*) : little house.

aedificium, -ii (*n.*) : building.

aedilis, -is (*m.*) : city magistrate.

aeger, -gra, -grum : ill.

aegritudo, -dinis (*f.*) : illness, ill-health.

aegroto, -are, -avi, -atum (*v.i.*) : be ill.

aegrotus, -a, -um : ill.

aequalitas, -tatis (*f.*) : equality, accuracy.

aequus, -a, -um : equal, fair, level.

aēr, -is (*acc.* **aëra**), (*m.*) : air, sky.

aestas, -atis (*f.*) : summer.

aestas, -ūs (*m.*) : heat, tide.

aetas, -atis (*f.*) : age.

aevum, -i (*n.*) : age, life, lifetime.

affectus (*p.p.* of **afficio**) : affected, disposed, indisposed.

affero, -ferre, attuli, allatum (*v.t.*) : bring.

affligo, -ere, -flixi, -flictum (*v.t.*) : afflict, trouble, lay low.

affulgeo, -ēre, -fulsi (*v.i.*) : shine, dawn.

ager, -gri (*m.*) : field, country.

agger, -eris (*m.*) : rampart, dyke.

agito, -are, -avi, -atum (*v.t.*) : keep moving, hold, discuss.

agnosco, -ere, -novi, -nitum (*v.t.*) : recognise.

ago, -ere, egi, -actum (*v.t.*) : do, drive, spend (time), live, play a part.

aio (*defective v.*) : say.

alacer, -cris, -cre : vigorous, healthy.

albus, -a, -um : white.

alibi (*adv.*) : elsewhere.

alicubi (*adv.*) : anywhere.

alienus, -a, -um : someone else's.

alio (*adv.*) : to another place, in another direction.

alioqui (*adv.*) : otherwise.

aliquamdiu (*adv.*) : for some time.

aliquando (*adv.*) : at some time.

aliquanto (*adv.*) : somewhat.

aliquis, -quid (*pron.* or *adj.*) : someone, some.

aliquot (*indecl. adj.*) : some, several.

aliquoties (*adv.*) : sometimes.

aliquousque (*adv.*) : to some extent.

alloquor, -i, -locutus (*v.t.*) : address, speak to.

alo, -ere, alui, altum (*v.t.*) : feed, support.

alter, -era, -erum : another, a second, the other.

altitudo, -dinis (*f.*) : height, depth.

altus, -a, -um : high, deep.

amando, -are, -avi, -atum (*v.t.*) : send away.

amans, -ntis : loving; *adv.* amanter.

ambio, -ire, -ii, -itum (*v.t.*) : be ambitious for.

ambitio, -onis (*f.*) : ambition.

amantissime (*superl. adv.*) : most affectionately.

amarulentia, -ae (*f.*) : bitterness, offensive smell.

ambo, -ae, -o : both.

ambulatio, -onis (*f.*) : walking, walk.

ambulo, -are, -avi, -atum (*v.i.*) : walk.

amentia, -ae (*f.*) : madness.

amice (*adv.*) : in a friendly manner.

amicitia, -ae (*f.*) : friendship.

amitto, -ere, -misi, -missum (*v.t.*) : lose.

amo, -are, -avi, -atum (*v.t.*) : love, esteem.

amoenitas, -atis (*f.*) : pleasantness.

amor, -oris (*m.*) : love, esteem, regard.

amplector, -i, -plexus (*v.t.*) : embrace, favour, cherish.

amplus, -a, -um : ample, large, extensive.

amussis, -is (*f.*) : ruler.

an : or, whether (in questions).

anceps, -cipitis : doubtful, uncertain.

angelatus, -i (*m.*) : angel (coin).

angelicus, -a, -um : angelic.

anguilla, -ae (*f.*) : eel.

angulus, -i (*m.*) : angle, corner.

anhelus, -a, -um : out of breath, panting.

animus, -i (*m.*) : mind, spirit, courage.

annitor, -i, -nisus (*v.i.*) : strive, make an effort.

annoto, -are, -avi, -atum (*v.t.*) : annotate, write notes on.

annue (*adv.*) : yearly.

annus, -i (*m.*) : year.

ante (*prep.* with *acc.*, or *adv.*) before.

antea (*adv.*) : before, formerly.

antehac (*adv.*) : previously.

antepono -ere, -posui, -positum (*v.t.*) : prefer.

antequam (*conj.*) : before.

antiquus, -a, -um : ancient; **antiquior** : preferable, more desirable.

aperio, -ire, -ui, -rtum (*v.t.*) : open, disclose.

apparatus, -ūs (*m.*) : preparation (for a meal), 'spread.'

appello, -ere, -puli, -pulsum (*v.t. and i.*) : put to shore, land.

appono, -ere, -posui, -positum (*v.t.*) : place before, serve (food).

approbo, -are, -avi, -atum (*v.t.*) : approve, favour, prove.

aptus, -a, -um : fit, suitable.

apud (*prep.* with *acc.*) : at, among, at the house of, near.

aqua, -ae (*f.*) : water.

arbitror, -ari, -atus (*v.i.*) : think.

arcanum, -i (*n.*) : secret.

arceo, -ēre, -cui (*v.t.*) : keep off, keep out.

Archidiaconus, -i (*m.*) : Archdeacon.

Archiepiscopus, -i (*m.*) : Archbishop.

ardeo, -ēre, arsi, arsum (*v.i.*) : be on fire, be eager.

ardor, -oris (*m.*) : ardour, burning enthusiasm.

arefacio, -ěre, -feci, -factum (*v.t.*): dry.

argilla, -ae (*f.*): clay.

argumentum, -i (*n.*): evidence, proof, subject--matter.

armatus, -i (*m.*): armed man.

arrideo, ēre, -risi, -risum (*v.i.*): smile upon (*lit.*), be favourable or acceptable.

arroganter (*adv.*): conceitedly, presumptuously.

arx, arcis (*f.*): castle.

ascendo, -ere, -ndi, -nsum (*v.i.* or *t.*): climb up, mount, rise.

ascribo, -ere, -psi, -ptum (*v.t.*): add (in writing).

asper, -a, -um: harsh, inclement.

aspernor, -ari, -atus (*v.t.*): disdain, despise, reject.

assequor, -sequi, -secutus (*v.t.*): attain, achieve.

assevero, -are, -avi, -atum (*v.t.*): affirm, maintain.

assiduitas, -atis (*f.*): continual work.

assiduus, -a, -um: hardworking, busy, incessant.

asto, -stare, -stiti, -stitum (*v.i.*): stand near.

at: but.

athleta, -ae (*com.*): wrestler, prizefighter.

atque: and.

atqui (*adv.*): and yet.

atrox, -ocis: fierce, frightful.

attente (*adv.*): carefully.

attingo, -ere, -tigi, -tactum (*v.t.*): touch, reach.

auctor, -oris (*m.*): author, adviser, suggester.

auctoritas, -atis (*f.*): authority, influence.

audio, -ire, -ivi, -itum (*v.t.*): hear, listen to.

aufero, -ferre, abstuli, ablatum (*v.t.*): remove.

auguror, -ari, -atus (*v.i.*): surmise, conjecture.

aula, -ae (*f.*): royal court.

aulicus, -i (*m.*): courtier.

aura, -ae (*f.*): breeze.

aureus, -a, -um: golden.

aurifaber, -bri (*m.*): goldsmith.

auriga, -ae (*m.*): coachman.

auris, -is (*f.*): ear.

aurum, -i (*n.*): gold.

auster, -tri (*m.*): south wind.

aut: either, or.

autem: but, moreover, however.

autumnus, -i (*m.*): autumn.

avis, -is (*f.*): bird.

avoco, -are, -avi, -atum: call away, distract.

baculum, -i (*n.*): stick.

beatus, -a, -um: happy.

belle (*adv.*): fairly, pretty.

bellicus, -a, -um: warlike.

bellum, -i (*n.*): war.

bellus, -a, -um: pretty, fine.

belua, -ae (*f.*): beast, monster.

bene (*adv.*): well.

beneficium, -i (*n.*): kindness, kindly act, help.

benevolentia, -ae (*f.*): kindness, well-wishing.

benigne (*adv.*): kindly, courteously.

benignitas, -atis (*f.*): friendliness, kindness.

biduum, -i (*n.*): (a period of) two days.

biga, -ae (*f.*): two-horsed coach.

bigarius, -i (*m.*): driver, coachman.

bilis, -is (*f.*): bile, biliousness; wrath, indignation.

blasphemo, -are, -avi, -atum (*v.t.*): slander, revile.

bombardicus pulvis: gunpowder.

bonitas, -atis (*f.*) : goodness.
Breve: a Papal Brief.
brevi (*adv.*) : in a short time.

cacumen, -inis (*n.*) : summit, top.
caduceator, -oris (*m.*) : herald.
caelum, i- (*n.*) : sky, weather, climate.
caenum, -i (*n.*) : mud.
caerimonia, -ae (*f.*) : ceremony, rite.
caerimoniola, -ae (*f.*) : petty ceremony.
calamus, .i (*m.*) : pen.
calcographus, -i (*m.*) : printer.
calculus, -i (*m.*) : stone, gall-stone.
caliendrum, -i (*n.*) : false hair, wig.
calx, calcis (*f.*) : bottom of a page.
camera, -ae (*f.*) : room, chamber.
Cancellarius, -i (*m.*) : Chancellor.
candeo, -ēre, -ui (*v.i.*) : to glow with heat, be red-hot.
candor, -oris (*m.*) : sincerity, frankness.
cano, -ere, cecini, cantum (*v.i.*) : to sing.
canonicus, -i (*m.*) : Canon.
cantharus, -i (*m.*) : tankard.
Canticum Canticorum: the Song of Songs.
cantor, -oris (*m.*) : singer, Precentor.
canus, -a, -um: white-headed; as *noun*, old man.
capillus, -i (*m.*) : hair.
capio, -ēre, cepi, captum: take, hold, contain.
capitalis, -e: fatal.
capitium, ii (*n.*) : hood.

caput, -itis (*n.*) : head, heading (of a letter).
carmen, -inis (*n.*) : song, poem.
carpa, -ae (*f.*) : carp.
carus, -a, -um: dear, beloved.
castigo, -are, -avi, -atum (*v.t.*) : chastise.
casus, -ūs (*m.*) : chance, happening, misfortune.
catastrophe (*f.*) : climax.
catechumenus, -i (*m.*) : candidate for Confirmation; see note.
cathedra, -ae (*f.*) : Bishop's throne, teacher's chair, armchair.
causa, -ae (*f.*) : reason.
cedo, -ere, cessi, cessum (*v.t.* and *i.*) : yield, fall short, give place to.
celebro, -are, -avi, -atum (*v.t.*) : celebrate, keep a festival.
celer, -ens: swift.
celsitudo, -inis (*f.*) : loftiness, Highness.
cena, -ae (*f.*) : dinner.
cenaculum, -i (*n.*) : dining-room.
ceno, -are, -avi, -atum (*v.i.*) : dine (*active p.p.* **cenatus**).
certamen, -inis (*n.*) : struggle, contest.
certe (*adv.*) : certainly, surely, at any rate.
certus, -a, -um: definite, sure, trustworthy.
cervisia, -ae (*f.*) : ale, beer.
cervisiarius, -a, -um: made with ale or beer.
cervisiola, -ae (*f.*) : light ale, small beer.
cesso, -are, -avi, -atum (*v.i.*) : slacken, cease.
ceteri, -ae, -a: the rest, the others.
ceterum (*adv.*) : however, but.

ceu (*adv.*) : as if, like.

Chaos (*n.*) : empty space, Chaos.

charta, -ae (*f.*) : paper.

chartaceus, -a, -um : made or consisting of paper.

chartarius, -a, -um : connected with paper.

chirurgus, -i (*m.*) : surgeon.

cibus, -i (*m.*) : food.

cinericius, -a, -um : of the colour of ashes, ashen.

circa (*adv.* and *prep.*) : about, round about.

circumfundo, -ere, -fudi, -fusum (*v.t.*) : surround.

citra (*prep.* with *acc.*) : this side of, short of.

civitas, -atis (*f.*) : state, city.

clamito, -are, -avi, -atum (*v.i.*) : shout, bawl.

clamor, -oris (*m.*) : shouting.

clarus, -a, -um : famous, distinguished.

classis, -is (*f.*) : fleet, class.

claudo, -ere, -si, -sum (*v.t.*) : shut.

claudus, -a, -um : lame.

clepsydra, -ae (*f.*) : water-clock.

clientulus, -i (*m.*) : humble client.

cloaca, -ae (*f.*) : sewer.

codex, -icis (*m.*) : manuscript.

coemeterium, -i (*n.*) : cemetery.

coeo, -ire, -ii, -itum (*v.i.*) : come together, join up.

coepi, -isse (*v.i.*) : I began, have begun.

coerceo, -ēre, -cui, -citum (*v.t.*) : restrain, keep in check.

cogito, -are, -avi, -atum (*v.i.*) : think.

cognitio, -onis (*f.*) : knowledge.

cognomen, -inis (*n.*) : surname.

cognomentum, -i (*n.*) : surname, name.

cognosco, -ere, -novi, -nitum (*v.t.*) : get to know, find out.

cogo, -ere, coegi, coactum (*v.t.*) : compel, gather.

colatus, *p.p.* of colare : filtered.

collatio, -onis (*f.*) : comparison.

collegialis, -is : connected with a college.

collegium, -ii (*n.*) : college.

colloco, -are, -avi, -atum (*v.t.*) : place, arrange.

colloquium, -ii (*n.*) : conversation.

colluctor, -ari, -atus (*v.i.*) : wrestle.

colluvies (*f.*) : medley, motley collection, off-scourings.

color, -oris (*m.*) : colour.

Comes, -itis (*m.*) : Count.

comissor, -ari, -atus (*v.i.*) : make merry, carouse, feast.

comiter (*adv.*) : politely, friendly, affably.

comitor, -ari, -atus (*v.t.*) : accompany.

commendatio, -onis (*f.*) : recommendation.

commendo, -ari, -avi, -atum (*v.t.*) : recommend.

commentarius, -i (*m.*) : commentary.

commentatio, -onis (*f.*) : commentary.

commentor, -ari, -atus (*v.i.*) : meditate, consider.

commercor, -ari, -atus (*v.t.*) : purchase.

commisceo, -ēre, -ui, -xtum (*v.t.*) : mix, mingle.

committo, -ere, -misi, -missum (*v.t.*) : entrust.

commode (*adv.*) : suitably, pleasantly.

commoditas, -atis (*f.*) : convenience, courtesy.

commodus, -a, -um: appropriate, friendly, obliging, useful.

communico, -are, -avi, -atum (*v.t.*): share, impart.

communis, -is: common, general.

commuto, -are, -avi, -atum (*v.t.*): change.

compater, -tris (*m.*): godfather.

comperio, -ire, comperi, compertum (*v.i.*): discover.

complector, -i, -xus (*v.t.*): embrace, care for.

complures, -plurium: several.

complusculi: several.

compono, -ere, -posui, -positum (*v.t.*): put together, arrange, settle.

conatus, -ūs (*m.*): attempt, undertaking.

concedo, -ere, -cessi, -cessum (*v.t.* and *i.*): yield, withdraw.

concilio, -are, -avi, -atum (*v.t.*): win the favour of, win over.

concinno, -are, -avi, -atum (*v.t.*): make tidy.

concipio, -ĕre, -cepi, -ceptum (*v.t.*): gather, accumulate.

conclave, -is (*n.*): room.

concordia, -ae (*f.*): agreement, harmony.

concurro, -ere, -curri, -cursum (*v.i.*): make an attack.

concutio, -ĕre, -cussi, -cussum (*v.t.*): shatter.

condicio, -onis (*f.*): condition, terms.

condo, -ere, -didi, -ditum (*v.t.*): found, build.

condono, -are, -avi, -atum (*v.t.*): pardon.

conduco, -ere, -xi, -ctum (*v.t.*): hire.

confabulor, -ari, -atus (*v.i.*): talk, chat.

confero, -ferre, -tuli, -latum (*v.t.*): bring together, compare; **se conferre**: go.

confestim (*adv.*): immediately, speedily.

conficio, -ĕre, -feci, -fectum (*v.t.*): finish, wear out, exhaust.

confido, -ere, -fisus sum (with *dative*): trust.

confoveo, -ĕre, -fovi, -fotum (*v.t.*): warm.

confrater, -tris (*m.*): Brother (in a monastery).

congero, -ere, -gessi, -gestum (*v.t.*): pile up, build, collect, compile.

congius, -i (*m.*): Roman liquid measure, nearly a gallon.

congressus, -ūs (*m.*): encounter, fight.

congruo, -ui (*v.i.*): agree, be suited to.

conicio, -ĕre, -ieci, -iectum (*v.t.* and *i.*): hurl, conjecture, guess.

coniungo, -ere, -nxi, -nctum (*v.t.*): join, connect.

coniunx, -iugis (*com.*): wife or husband.

conor, -ari, -atus (*v.i.*): try.

conquiesco, -ere, -quievi, -quietum (*v.i.*): be at rest, die down.

conscendo, -ere, -ndi, -nsum (*v.t.*): mount.

consentio, -ire, -sensi, -sensum (*v.i.*): agree.

consequor, -i, -secutus (*v.t.*): overtake, attain.

consilium, -i (*n.*): plan, advice, wisdom, strategy.

consolor, -ari, -atus (*v.t.*): comfort, cheer.

conspergo, -ere, -si, -sum (*v.t.*): sprinkle.

conspicio, -ĕre, -spexi, -spectum (*v.t.*) : catch sight of.

constanter (*adv.*) : firmly, stoutly.

consterno, -are, -avi, -atum (*v.t.*) : alarm.

consterno, -ere, -stravi, -stratum (*v.t.*) : strew, pave.

consto, -are, -stiti, -statum (*v.i.*) : cost.

construo, -ere, -strui, -structum (*v.t.*) : build.

consuesco, -ere, -suevi, -suetum (*v.i.*) : be accustomed.

consuetedo, -dinis (*f.*) : society, acquaintance.

consulo, -ere, -sului, -sultum (*v.t.*) : consult; (with *dative*) have regard for, look to.

consumo, -ere, -sumpsi, -sumptum (*v.t.*) : consume, destroy, waste.

contemno, -ere, -tempsi, -temptum (*v.t.*) : despise.

contemplor, -ari, -atus (*v.t.*) : gaze at.

contemptus, -ūs (*m.*) : contempt, scorn.

contendo, -ere, -ndi, -ntum (*v.i.*) : hasten, journey, strive.

continens, -tis (*f.*) : continent.

contineo, -ēre, -ui, -tentum (*v.t.*) : contain, keep in check.

contingo, -ere, -tigi, -tactum (*v.t.* and *i.*) : touch, reach; contingit : it falls to one's lot.

contionor, -ari, -atum (*v.i.*) : make a speech, preach.

contra (*adv.* and *prep.* with *acc.*) : on the contrary, against.

contraho, -ere, -traxi, -tractum (*v.t.*) : gather together.

contubernium, -ii)*n.*) : society.

contundo, -ere, -tudi, -tusum (*v.t.*): beat, belabour.

convalesco, -ere, -valui (*v.i.*): get well, recover.

convenio, -ire, -veni, -ventum (*v.t.* and *i.*) : meet, be suitable, seemly.

conventus, -ūs (*m.*) : meeting, gathering.

convicium, -ii (*n.*) : abuse, insult.

convivator, -oris (*m.*) : master of a feast, host.

convivium, -ii (*m.*) : feast, banquet.

copulo, -are, -avi, -atum (*v.t.*) : join, associate.

coram (*adv.* and *prep.* with *abl.*) : in the presence of, publicly, face to face.

cordatus, -a, -um : prudent, judicious.

coronatus, -i (*n.*) : crown (coin).

corpusculum, -i (*n.*) : frail body.

corripio, -ĕre, -ui, -reptum (*v.t.*) : take hold of.

cotidie (*adv.*) = quotidie : daily.

coxa, -ae (*f.*) : hip.

crapula, -ae (*f.*) : intoxication.

creber, -bra, -brum : frequent, numerous.

credo, -ere, -didi, -ditum (*v.t.* and *i.*) : believe.

crepitus, -ūs (*m.*) : clatter, crash.

cruciatus, -ūs (*m.*) : torture, excruciating pain.

crudelis, -is : cruel.

crudus, -a, -um : raw, uncooked.

cruentus, -a, -um : bloody, gory.

cubiculum, -i (*n.*) : bedroom.

cubo, -are, -ui, -itum : lie down, go to bed.

cucullus, -i (*m.*) : cowl.

culpa, -ae (*f.*) : fault, blame.

cultus, -ūs (*m.*) : dress, (monastic) habit.

cum (*conj.*) : when, whenever, since, although.

cum . . . tum: both . . . and; not only . . . but also.

cum (*prep.* with *abl.*) : with.

cupio, -ĕre, -ivi, -itum (*v.t.*) : desire.

curo, -are, -avi, -atum (*v.t.*) : look after ; (with *gerundive*), get a thing done.

currus, -ūs (*m.*) : coach, carriage.

cursus, -ūs (*m.*) : course, journey.

cynanche, -ēs (*f.*) : sore throat, quinsy.

damno, -are, -avi, -atum (*v.t.*) : condemn.

damnum, -i (*n.*) : damage, loss.

deambulatiuncula, -ae (*f.*) : stroll.

deambulo, -are, -avi, -atum (*v.i.*) : walk, stroll.

debeo, -ēre, -ui, -itum (*v.t.* and *i.*) : ought, owe.

Decanus, -i (*m.*) : Dean.

decerno, -ere, -crevi, -cretum (*v.i.*) : decree, decide.

declaro, -are, -avi, -atum (*v.t.*) : declare, prove, show.

decumbo, -ere, -cubui, -cubitum (*v.i.*) : lie ill in bed.

deduco, -ere, -xi, -ctum (*v.t.*) : escort.

deficio, -ĕre, -feci, -fectum (*v.t.* and *i.*) : fail.

defleo, -ēre, -flevi, -fletum (*v.t.*) : bewail.

defraudo, -are, -avi, -atum (*v.t.*) : cheat, deprive.

defunctus (*p.p.* defungor) : dead.

deinde (*adv.*) : then, next.

delecto, -are, -avi, -atum (*v.t.*) : delight, please.

delectus, -ūs (*m.*) : choice, selection.

deliciae, -arum (*f.*) : delights, pleasures.

deligo, -ere, -legi, -lectum (*v.t.*) : choose.

delitesco, -ere, -litui (*v.i.*) : hide, conceal oneself.

demando, -are, -avi, -atum (*v.t.*) : entrust.

demereor, -ēri, -itus (*v.t.*) : lay under an obligation, oblige.

demigro, -are, -avi, -atum (*v.i.*) : depart.

demitto, -ere, -misi, -missum (*v.t.*) : to send down, lower.

demiror, -ari, -atus (*v.t.*) : wonder at.

demolior, -iri, -itus (*v.t.*) : demolish.

denique (*adv.*) : finally, in short.

denuo (*adv.*) : afresh, again.

depello, -ere, -puli, -pulsum (*v.t.*) : ward off.

depono, -ere, -posui, -positum (*v.t.*) : lift down, lay aside.

deprehendo, -ere, -ndi, -nsum (*v.t.*) : catch, detect.

depugno, -are, -avi, -atum (*v.i.*) : fight.

descendo, -ere, -ndi, -nsum (*v.t.*) : climb down, dismount.

describo, -ere, -psi, -ptum (*v.t.*) : describe, write out.

desideo, -ēre, -sedi, -sessum (*v.i.*) : sit idle.

desiderium, -ii (*n.*) : longing, parting, separation.

desidero, -are, -avi, -atum (*v.t.*) : long for, desire.

designo, -are, -avi, -atum (*v.t.*) : describe, arrange, appoint.

despero, -are, -avi, -atum (*v.i.*) : despair.

destinor, -ari, destinatus (*v.t.*) : choose, fix, aim at.

destituo, -ere, -ui, -utum (*v.t.*) : abandon, desert.

desum, -esse, -fui (v.i.): be lacking, fail.

detineo, -ēre, -ui, -tentum (v.t.): keep back.

detraho, -ere, -xi, -ctum (v.t.): drag off.

devincio, -ire, -nxi, -nctum (v.t.): lay under an obligation.

dexter, -tra, -trum: right.

dextra, -ae (f.): right hand.

dico, -ere, -xi, -ctum (v.t.): say.

dictio, -onis (f.): expression, word.

dictum, -i (n.): saying.

diduco, -ere, -xi, -ctum (v.t.): draw apart.

differo, -ferre, distuli, dilatum (v.t.): differ, postpone.

difficilis, -is: difficult.

diffido, -ere, -fisus sum (v. with dat.): distrust.

dignus, -a, -um: worthy, suitable.

dilectus, -a, -um: beloved.

diligenter (adv.): carefully.

diligentia, -ae (f.): care, diligence.

diligo, -ere, -lexi, -lectum (v.t.): love, value.

diminuo, -ere, -ui, -utum (v.t.): lessen, take from.

dimitto, -ere, -misi, -missum (v.t.): send away.

dirimo, -ere, -emi, -emptum (v.t.): separate.

discedo, -ere, -cessi, -cessum (v.i.): depart.

discessus, -ūs (m.): departure.

disciplina, -ae (f.): teaching, learning, knowledge.

discipulus, -i (m.): pupil.

disco, -ere, didici (v.t.): learn.

discrimen, -inis (n.): danger, crisis.

dispensator, -oris (m.): steward, treasurer.

dispenso, -are, -avi, -atum (v.t.): dispense, pay out.

disputo, -are, -avi, -atum (v.i.): discuss, argue.

dissimulo, -are, -avi, -atum (v.t.): disguise, hide.

dissolvo, -ere, -solvi, -solutum (v.t.): pay, change money.

dissuadeo, -ēre, -suasi, -suasum (v.t.): dissuade.

distentus (p.p. distineo): busy, occupied.

distinguo, -ere, -nxi, -nctum (v.t.): divide, separate.

distorqueo, -ēre, -si, -tum (v.t.): twist, wrench.

distribuo, -ere, -ui, -utum (v.t.): distribute.

distringo, -ere, -nxi, -ctum (v.t.): distract, preoccupy.

diutinus, -a, -um: long-lasting.

diversorium, -ii (m.): inn.

diversus, -a, -um: different, contrary, opposite.

diverto, -ere, -ti, -sum (v.i.): lodge at an inn.

divino, -are, -avi, -atum (v.t.): predict.

divinus, -a, -um: divine, holy.

divortium, -ii (n.): divorce, separation.

divus, -a, -um: saintly, Saint.

doceo, -ēre, -ui, -ctum (v.t.): teach, explain.

doctor, -oris (m.): Doctor (of Theology, etc.).

doctus (p.p. doceo): learned.

doctrina, -ae (f.): learning.

doleo, -ēre, -ui (v.t.): grieve, mourn for.

dolor, -oris (m.): grief, pain.

domesticus, -a, -um: domestic, private.

domina, -ae (f.): mistress.

dominus, -i (m.): master.

Dominicus dies: Sunday (French 'Dimanche').

domuncula, -ae (*f.*): little house.

domus, -ūs (*f.*): house.

donec (*conj.*): until.

dono, -are, -avi, -atum (*v.t.*): give, present.

donum, -i (*n.*): gift.

dormio, -ire, -ii or **-ivi, -itum** (*v.i.*): sleep.

dormito, -are, -avi, -atum (*v.i.*): sleep, doze.

dorsum, -i (*n.*): back.

dubito, -are, -avi, -atum (*v.t.* and *i.*): doubt, hesitate.

ducenti, -ae, -a: two hundred.

dulcedo, -inis (*f.*): pleasure.

dulcis, -is: sweet, pleasant.

duntaxat (*adv.*): only.

dum (*conj.*): while, until, provided that.

duplus, -a, -um: double.

duratus, -a, -um: hardened.

ecce!: lo and behold!

ēditio, -onis (*f.*): edition.

ĕdo, edere, edi, esum (*v.t.*): eat.

ēdo, -ere, -didi, -ditum (*v.t.*): publish, reveal.

educo, -are -avi, -atum (*v.t.*): educate.

effero, -ferre, extuli, elatum (*v.t.*): carry out, bury.

efficax, -acis: efficient.

effodio, -ere, -fodi, -fossum (*v.t.*): dig out.

effugio, -ĕre, -fugi, -fugitum (*v.i.*): escape.

effulgeo, -ēre, -fulsi, -fulsum (*v.i.*): shine out, flash.

effundo, -ere, -fūdi, -fusum (*v.t.*): pour out.

egredior, -i, -gressus (*v.i.*): go out.

egregius, -ia, -ium: excellent, remarkable, eminent.

eicio, -ĕre, -ieci, -iectum (*v.t.*): cast out, put on shore.

elegantia, -ae (*f.*): refinement, civilisation.

emico, -are, -ui, -atum (*v.i.*): flash out.

eminens, -tis: lofty, raised.

emo, -ere, emi, emptum (*v.t.*): buy.

encomium, -ii (*n.*): praise, eulogy.

eneco, -are, -ui, -ctum (*v.t.*): kill off.

energia, -ae (*f.*): power, efficacy.

enim: for.

enitor, -i, -nisus (*v.i.*): make an effort.

episcopus, -i (*m.*): bishop.

epistola, -ae (*f.*): letter.

epistolium, -ii (*n.*): note.

epulae, -arum (*f.*): feast.

equidem = ego quidem: I for my part.

equitatio, -onis (*f.*): riding, ride.

equus, -i (*m.*): horse.

erga (*prep.* with *acc.*): towards (people).

ergo (*adv.*): therefore.

erigo, -ere, -rexi, -rectum (*v.t.*): raise up.

eripio, -ĕre, -ripui, -reptum (*v.t.*): seize, snatch.

error, -oris (*m.*): mistake.

erudio, -ire, -ii, -itum (*v.t.*): teach.

eruditio, -onis (*f.*): learning.

eruditus, -a, -um: learned, well-educated.

eruo, -ere, -rui, -rutum (*v.t.*): dig out, extract.

et: and, also, even; **et ... et**: both ... and.

etiam: even, also.

etiamnum: even now, still.

evado, -ere, -vasi, -vasum (v.t. and i.): escape.

evello, -ere, -velli, -vulsum (v.t.): tear out.

evoco, -are, -avi, -atum (v.t.): call out, call forth.

exacerbo, -are, -avi, -atum (v.t.): make angry, aggravate.

exacte (adv.): precisely, accurately.

exaspero, -are, -avi, -atum (v.t.): roughen, make harsh.

excedo, -ere, -cessi, -cessum (v.i.): go out, depart.

excido, -ere, -cidi (v.i.): fall from, be disappointed in.

excipio, -ĕre, -cepi, -ceptum (v.t.): take, receive.

excito, -are, -avi, -atum (v.t.): rouse.

excludo, -ere, -clusi, -clusum (v.t.): shut out.

excuso, -are, -avi, -atum (v.t.): plead as an excuse.

exemplum, -i (n.): copy.

exerceo, -ēre, -ui, -itum (v.t.): practise, harass, plague.

exercito, -are, -avi, -atum (v.t.): practise.

exhalo, -are, -avi, -atum (v.t.): breathe out, give off vapour.

exhibeo, -ēre, -ui, -itum (v.t.): show, display.

exigo, -ere, -egi, -actum (v.t.): demand.

exiguus, -a, -um: scanty, tiny.

exitium, -ii (n.): destruction.

exitus, -ūs (m.): departure, death.

exorior, -iri, -ortus (v.i.): arise.

expergiscor, -i, -perrectus (v.i.): wake up, come to.

expleo, -ēre, -plevi, -pletum (v.t.): fill up, stuff.

explico, -are, -avi, -atum (v.t.): explain, express.

exploro, -are, -avi, -atum (v.t.): search.

exspatior, -ari, -atus (v.i.): go for a walk.

exspecto, -are, -avi, -atum (v.t.): wait for, expect.

exstinguo, -ere, -nxi, -nctum (v.t.): extinguish, kill.

exstruo, -ere, -xi, -ctum (v.t.): build.

extorqueo, -ēre, -torsi, -tortum (v.t.): extort, wrest.

extremus, -a, -um: furthest, utmost.

extrudo, -ere, -si, -sum (v.t.): thrust out.

extundo, -ere, -tudi, -tusum (v.t.): drive out.

exturbo, -are, -avi, -atum (v.t.): drive out, turn out.

faber, -bri (m.): smith, blacksmith.

fabula, -ae (f.): story.

facies, -ei (f.): face, expression, appearance.

facile (adv.): easily.

facio, -ĕre, feci, factum (v.t.): do, make.

factito, -are, -avi, -atum (v.t.): do frequently.

fallo, -ere, fefelli, falsum (v.t.): cheat, deceive.

familia, -ae (f.): family, household.

familiaris, -is (m. or f.): friend.

familiariter (adv.): familiarly, intimately.

familiaritas, -atis (f.): friendship, intimacy.

famulus, -a: man- or maidservant.

fas (indecl. n.): right.

fastidium, -ii (*n.*): dislike, aversion.

fateor, -ēri, fassus (*v.t.*): confess, admit.

faustus, -a, -um: fortunate, lucky.

faveo, -ēre, fāvi, fautum (*v.* with *dat.*): favour, be well-disposed to.

febricito, -are, -avi, -atum (*v.i.*): feel feverish.

febricula, -ae (*f.*): slight fever.

febris, -is (*f.*): fever.

felicitas, -atis (*f.*): happiness.

feliciter (*adv.*): happily, luckily.

felix, -icis: happy.

fenestra, -ae (*f.*): window.

fere, ferme (*adv.*): almost, about, generally.

ferio, -ire [percussi, percussum] (*v.t.*): strike.

fero, ferre, tuli, latum (*v.t.*): carry, bring, produce, endure; prae se ferre: display.

ferocia, -ae (*f.*): ferocity, savageness.

ferreus, -a, -um: made of iron.

ferrum, -i (*n.*): iron, steel, weapon.

festino, -are, -avi, -atum (*v.i.*): hasten.

fetor, -oris (*m.*): stench.

fides, -ei (*f.*): loyalty, belief, trustworthiness.

fido, -ere, fisus sum (*v.* with *dat.*): trust.

fidus, -a, -um: loyal, trustworthy.

figo, -ere, -xi, -xum (*v.t.*): fix.

finio, -ire, -ivi, -itum (*v.t.*): finish.

finis, -is (*m.*): end.

fio, fieri, factus (*v.i.*): become, be made.

firmus, -a, -um: strong, robust.

flammeum, -i (*n.*): veil.

fleo, -ēre, flevi, fletum (*v.t.* and *i.*): weep, lament.

flo, -are, -avi, -atum (*v.i.*): blow.

florenus, -i (*m.*): florin.

floreo, -ēre, florui (*v.i.*): flourish.

flumen, -inis (*n.*): river.

foculus, -i (*m.*): brazier, stove.

foedus, -a, -um: filthy, foul.

foedus, -eris (*n.*): treaty.

formido, -are, -avi, -atum (*v.t.*): fear.

fortasse, fortassis (*adv.*): perhaps.

forte (*adv.*): by chance.

fortiter (*adv.*): bravely.

fortitudo, -inis (*f.*): bravery, courage.

fortuna, -ae (*f.*): fortune, chance.

fossa, -ae (*f.*): ditch.

foveo, -ēre, fovi, fotum (*v.t.*): warm.

fragmentum, -i (*n.*): piece.

fragor, -oris (*m.*): crash.

frango, -ere, fregi, fractum (*v.t.*): break.

frequens, -tis: crowded, wide-spread.

frequenter (*adv.*): often.

fretus, -a, -um: relying on (with *abl.*).

frigidus, -a, -um: cold, dull.

fructus, -ūs (*m.*): fruit, produce, result, profit.

frugifer, -a, -um: fruitful, profitable.

fruor, frui, fructus (*v.* with *abl.*): enjoy, reap the fruits of.

frustra (*adv.*): in vain.

fugio, -ĕre, fugi, fugitum (*v.t.* and *i.*): escape, shun.

fugito, -are, -avi, -atum (*v.t.*): flee from, shun.

fulgor, -oris (*m.*): brightness, bright light.

fulmen, -inis (*n.*): thunderbolt.
fumus, -i (*m.*): smoke.
fundamentum, -i (*n.*): foundation, floor.
fundus, -i (*m.*): farm.
furtim (*adv.*): stealthily.
fuse (*adv.*): copiously, fully.
fustis, -is (*m.*): cudgel.
futurum, -i (*n.*): future.

gaudeo, -ēre, gavisus sum (*v.i.*): rejoice.
gaudium, -ii (*n.*): joy.
generosus, -a, -um: noble.
genetrix, -tricis (*f.*): mother.
genus, -eris (*n.*): kind, sort.
geometricus, -a, -um: geometrical.
gero, -ere, gessi, gestum (*v.t.*): carry, wage; **se gerere**: behave oneself.
gestio, -ire, -ii, -itum (*v.i.*): be joyful, jump for joy.
gesto, -are, -avi, -atum (*v.t.*): carry.
gestus, -ūs (*m.*): gesture, attitude.
gigno, -ere, genui, genitum (*v.t.*): produce, beget.
glaucoma, -atis (*n.*): blindness, dizziness.
glebula, -ae (*f.*): clod of turf or peat.
glomus, -eris (*n.*): ball of wool, handful (of hair).
gradus, -ūs (*m.*): step.
graecor, -ari, -atus (*v.i.*): imitate the Greeks, study Greek.
grandis, -is: large.
gratia, -ae (*f.*): favour, popularity; **gratiae**: thanks.
gratuito (*adv.*): without pay, gratis.
gratuitus, -a, -um: free.
gratulor, -ari, -atus (*v.t.*): congratulate.

gratus, -a, -um: welcome, pleasing.
gravis, -is: heavy, serious, unpleasant.
graviter (*adv.*): seriously, gravely.
grex, gregis (*m.*): flock, company, throng.
gula, -ae (*f.*): gluttony.

habeo, -ēre, -ui, -itum (*v.t.*): have, hold, consider.
hactenus (*adv.*): hitherto.
haereo, -ēre, haesi, haesum (*v.i.*): stick, cling.
haudquaquam (*adv.*): by no means.
haurio, -ire, hausi, haustum (*v.t.*): drain, drink, derive.
hebdomas, -adis (*f.*): week.
hera, -ae (*f.*): mistress.
herba, -ae (*f.*): grass, herbage.
hereditas, -atis (*f.*): inheritance.
hic (*adv.*): here, hereupon.
hilaritas, -atis (*f.*): cheerfulness, merriment.
hilariter (*adv.*): merrily.
hinc (*adv.*): hence.
hio, -are, -avi, -atum (*v.i.*): yawn, gape.
honestus, -a, -um: honourable.
honorificenter (*adv.*): with respect.
honos, -oris (*m.*): honour, office.
hora, -ae (*f.*): hour.
horreo, -ēre, -ui (*v.t.*): shudder at, loathe.
horribilis, -is: awesome, terrifying.
hortatus, -ūs (*m.*): encouragement, advice.
hortensis, -is: of a garden.
hortor, -ari, -atus (*v.t.*): urge, exhort.
hortus, -i (*m.*): garden.

hospes, -itis (*m.*): host, inn-keeper.

hospitium, -ii (*n.*): hospitality, hostel, inn.

huc (*adv.*): hither.

humanitas, -atis (*f.*): kindness, culture.

humanus, -a, -um: human, humane, cultured.

humerus, -i (*m.*): shoulder.

humilis, -is: humble, of short stature.

humus, -i (*f.*): earth, ground.

hymnus, -i (*m.*): hymn.

hypocaustum, -i (*n.*): sweating-chamber (*see* note).

hypodidasculus, -i (*m.*): under-master.

ibi: there.

idolatria, -ae (*f.*): idolatry.

igitur: therefore.

ignis, -is (*m.*): fire.

ilex, -icis (*f.*): holm-oak.

ilico (*adv.*): on the spot, immediately.

illabor, -i, -lapsus (*v.i.*): slip in.

illic (*adv.*): there.

illinc (*adv.*): from there.

illuc (*adv.*): thither.

illustro, -are, -avi, -atum (*v.t.*): shed light upon, illuminate.

imbecillitas, -atis (*f.*): weakness, frailty.

imbecillus, -a, -um: frail, feeble.

imber, -bris (*m.*): shower of rain.

imbuo, -ere, -ui, -utum (*v.t.*): instruct.

immanis, -is: enormous, inhuman.

immerens, -tis: undeserving.

immigro, -are, -avi, -atum (*v.i.*): remove oneself, go into.

immineo, -ēre (*v.i.*): hang over, be above, threaten.

immo (*adv.*): nay rather (correcting or emphasising previous statement).

immorior, -mori, -mortuus (*v.i.*): die.

impatiens, -tis: unable to endure (with *gen.*).

impedio, -ire, -ii or -ivi, -itum (*v.t.*): hinder, prevent.

Imperialis, -is: Imperial, of the Emperor.

impetro, -are, -avi, -atum (*v.t. and i.*): gain (by asking), secure.

impetus, -ūs (*m.*): attack, impulse.

impingo, -ere, -pegi, -pactum (*v.t.*): strike.

impono, -ere, -posui, -positum (*v.t.*): place upon, impose on (with *dat.*).

impressio, -onis (*f.*): impression, printing.

impressor, -oris (*m.*): printer.

imprimo, -ere, -pressi, -pressum (*v.t.*): print.

improbus, -a, -um: wicked, persistent.

impune (*adv.*): with impunity, unpunished.

imputo, -are, -avi, -atum (*v.t.*): ascribe, impute.

imus, -a, -um: lowest, bottom of.

inaedificio, -are, -avi, -atum (*v.t.*): build.

inaestimabilis, -is: incalculable.

inamoenus, -a, -um: unpleasant.

inanis, -is: empty.

incalesco, -ere, -calui (*v.i.*): grow heated.

incenatus, -a, -um: not having dined.

incendium, -ii (*n.*): fire, conflagration.

incessus, -ūs (*m.*): act of walking, gait, pace.

incido, -ere, -cĭdi, -casum (*v.i.*): fall upon, light upon.

incipio, -ĕre, -cepi, -ceptum (*v.t. and i.*): begin.

inclinatus, -a, -um: prone to.

incogitans, -tis: thoughtless, inconsiderate.

incogitantia, -ae (*f.*): thoughtlessness.

incognitus, -a, -um: unknown.

incola, -ae (*com.*): inhabitant.

incolumis, -is: safe, unharmed.

incommode (*adv.*): unfortunately.

incommodum, -i (*n.*): inconvenience, trouble.

incommodus, -a, -um: unsuitable, troublesome, awkward.

inconsultus, -a, -um: thoughtless, indiscreet.

incredibilis, -is: unbelievable.

incuria, -ae (*f.*): heedlessness.

incurvatus, -a, -um: bent over.

inde (*adv.*): thence.

indigenus, -a, -um: native.

indoctus, -a, -um: unlearned.

indoles, -is (*f.*): natural ability, disposition, character.

induco, -ere, -xi, -ctum (*v.t.*): induce, persuade; introduce.

inedia, -ae (*f.*): abstaining from food, fasting.

ineptus, -a, -um: stupid.

infamo, -are, -avi, -atum (*v.t.*): defame, slander.

infans, -tis (*com.*): infant, baby.

infesto, -are, -avi, -atum (*v.t.*): attack, trouble.

inflecto, -ere, -flexi, -flexum (*v.t.*): bend.

ingenium, -ii (*n.*): intellect, talents.

ingens, -tis: huge.

ingravesco, -ere (*v.i.*): grow worse.

ingredior, -i, -gressus (*v.t. and i.*): enter, embark upon.

ingressus, -ūs (*m.*): entrance, gait.

inguen, -inis (*m.*): groin.

inhorresco, -ere, -horrui (*v.i.*): shudder, shiver.

inimicus, -a, -um: hostile, enemy.

iniquus, -a, -um: uneven, unfair.

innocuus, -a, -um: uninjured.

innumerus, -a, -um: countless.

inopia, -ae (*f.*): lack, scarcity.

inprimis (*adv.*): especially.

inquam, inquit (*defect. vb.*): I say, he says (or said).

insalutatus, -a, -um: ungreeted.

inscendo, -ere, -ndi, -nsum (*v.t.*): mount.

inscitia, -ae (*f.*): ignorance.

inscribo, -ere, -psi, -ptum (*v.t.*): dedicate.

insido, -ere, -sedi, -sessum (*v.t. and i.*): sit upon.

insigne, -is (*n.*): badge of office, or honour; 'degree.'

insignis, -is: remarkable, distinguished.

insomnis, -is: sleepless.

instituo, -ere, -ui, -utum (*v.t.*): begin, instruct, teach.

insto, -stare, -stiti, -statum (*v.i.*): urge, insist.

insuavis, -is: disagreeable.

insula, -ae (*f.*): island.

integer, -gra, -grum: entire, unhurt, honest.

intellego, -ere, -lexi, -lectum (*v.t.*): understand, realise.

inter (*prep.* with *acc.*): among, between.

intercessio, -onis (*f.*): mediation, good offices.

intereo, -ire, -ii, -itum (*v.i.*): die.

interim, interea (*adv.*): meanwhile, sometimes (interim).

intersectus (*p.p.* interseco): intersected.

intervallum, -i (*n.*): interval, space between.

intolerabilis, -is: unbearable.

intra (*prep.* with *acc.*): within, inside.

inuro, -ere, -ussi, -ustum (*v.t.*): burn, brand.

inutilis, -is: useless.

invado, -ere, -vasi, -vasum (*v.t.*): attack.

invalesco, -ere, -valui (*v.i.*): increase.

invicem (*adv.*): in turn.

invidia, -ae (*f.*): ill-will.

inviso, -ere, -si, -sum (*v.t.*): visit.

invito, -are, -avi, -atum (*v.t.*): invite.

invitus, -a, -um: unwilling.

involo, -are, -avi, -atum (*v.t.*): fly at, pounce upon.

ira, -ae (*f.*): anger.

irascor, -i, iratus (with *dat.*): get angry with.

irrumpo, -ere, -rupi, -ruptum (*v.t.* and *i.*): rush in.

iste, -a, istud: that (of yours).

istic (*adv.*): there.

itaque: therefore, and so.

item (*adv.*): likewise.

iter, itineris (*n.*): journey, route.

iterum (*adv.*): for a second time, again.

itidem (*adv.*): in like manner, in the same spirit.

itio, -onis (*f.*): going (opp. to reditio).

iaceo, -ēre, -ui (*v.i.*): lie down, lie ill.

iactantia, -ae (*f.*): boastfulness, bragging.

iactatio, -onis (*f.*): tossing, jolting.

iactito, -are, -avi, -atum (*v.t.*): toss, boast.

iacto, -are, -avi, -atum (*v.t.* and *i.*): toss, boast.

iactura, -ae (*f.*): sacrifice, loss.

iam (*adv.*): now, already, soon.

iamdudum (*adv.*): for some time now.

iampridem (*adv.*): for a long time.

ieiunium, -ii (*n.*): fasting, hunger.

iocus, -i (*m.*): joke, jest.

iubileus, -a, -um: Jubilee.

iucundus, -a, -um: pleasant.

iudex, -icis (*m.*): judge.

iudicium, -ii (*n.*): judgement, opinion.

iugulo, -are, -avi, -atum (*v.t.*): (literally) kill (*see* note).

iureconsultus, -i (*m.*): lawyer.

ius, iuris (*n.*): law, right.

iustus, -a, -um: just, fair.

iuvat (*impers. vb.*): it pleases.

iuvenis, -is (*m.*): young man.

iuxta (*prep.* with *acc.*): near, close to, in accordance with.

lăbor, -oris (*m.*): work, toil.

lābor, -i, lapsus (*v.i.*): slip, slide.

laboro, -are, -avi, -atum (*v.i.*): work, be in difficulty or trouble.

lacer, -era, -erum: torn, mangled.

lacesso, -ere, -ivi, -itum (*v.t.*): harass, provoke, challenge.

laetor, -ari, -atus (*v.i.*): rejoice.

laetus, -a, -um: glad.

laevus, -a, -um: left (opp. to right).

laicus, -a, -um: secular.

languidulus, -a, -um: rather feeble, poorly.

laniena, -ae (*f.*): butcher's shop, shambles.

lapis, -idis (*m.*): stone.

lassulus, -a, -um: somewhat exhausted.

latibulum, -i (*n.*): hiding-place, retreat.

latro, -onis (*m.*): robber, highwayman.

lătus, -eris (*n.*): side.

laudatio, -onis (*f.*): praise, eulogy.

laudo, -are, -avi, -atum (*v.t.*): praise.

lautus, -a, -um: elegant, sumptuous.

lectio, -onis (*f.*): reading.

lectus, -i (*m.*): bed.

legio, -onis (*f.*): legion.

lego, -ere, legi, lectum (*v.t.*): choose, read.

lenis, -is: gentle, slight.

lente (*adv.*): slowly.

lentus, -a, -um: slow.

letalis, -is: deadly, mortal.

levis, -is: light.

levo, -are, -avi, -atum (*v.t.*): raise up.

lex, legis (*f.*): law.

libellus, -i (*m.*): (little) book, pamphlet.

libens, -tis: willing; *adv.* libenter.

liber, -bri (*m.*): book.

liber, -era, -erum: free.

liberalis, -is: generous.

libero, -are, -avi, -atum (*v.t.*): set free.

libet, libuit (*impers. vb.* with *dat.*): it pleases, I like.

libra, -ae (*f.*): pound.

licentia, -ae (*f.*): freedom, licence.

licet, licuit (*impers. vb.* with *dat.*): it is allowed, I may; as *conj.*, although.

lignum, -i (*n.*): wood.

lingua, -ae (*f.*): tongue, language.

linteum, -ei (*n.*): linen robe.

linteus, -a, -um: made of linen.

linum, -i (*n.*): linen, linen clothes, flax.

litera, -ae (*f.*): letter (of the alphabet); *pl.* a letter (correspondence), literature.

literatus, -a, -um: well educated, man of letters.

litus, -oris (*n.*): shore.

locus, -i (*m.*): place.

longe (*adv.*): far, by far.

longus, -a, -um: long, tedious.

loquacitas, -atis (*f.*): garrulity.

loquor, -i, locutus (*v.i.*): speak.

lucubratio, -onis (*f.*): night-work, composition, writing.

ludo, -ere, lusi, lusum (*v.i.*): play.

ludus, -i (*m.*): game, school.

lumen, -inis (*n.*): light.

lusito, -are, -avi, -atum (*v.i.*): play about.

lutum, -i (*n.*): mud.

luxus, -ūs (*m.*): luxury, debauchery.

macero, -are, -avi, -atum (*v.t.*): soak, wash.

madeo, -ēre, -ui (*v.i.*): to be sodden, to drip.

magister, -tri (*m.*): schoolmaster, Master of Arts.

magistratus, -ūs (*m.*): magistrate, town councillor.

magnificus, -a, -um: splendid; *adv.* magnifice.

magnitudo, -inis (*f.*): size, greatness.

magnopere (*adv.*): greatly.

malignus, -a, -um: stingy, scanty.

malo, malle, malui (*v.t.* and *i.*): prefer.

malum, -i (*n.*): misfortune, illness.

malus, -a, -um: bad, evil.

mando, -are, -avi, -atum (*v.t.*): entrust.

mane (*adv.*): in the morning, early.

mantica, -ae (*f.*): bag, portmanteau.

manus, -ūs (*f.*): hand.

mare, -is (*n.*): sea.

marinus, -a, -um: of the sea, marine.

Mars, -tis (*m.*): God of War, battle.

materfamilias, matrisfamilias (*f.*): mistress of the house.

matrona, -ae (*f.*): matron, lady.

maturus, -a, -um: mature.

medicus, -i (*m.*): physician.

meditor, -ari, -atus (*v.t.* and *i.*): ponder over, meditate.

medius, -a, -um: middle (of).

membrum, -i (*n.*): limb.

memini, -isse (with *gen.*): remember.

memoria, -ae (*f.*): memory, recollection.

mens, -tis (*f.*): mind.

mensa, -ae (*f.*): table.

mensis, -is (*m.*): month.

mensula, -ae (*f.*): desk.

mercator, -oris (*m.*): merchant.

mereo, -ēre, -ui, -itum (*v.t.*): deserve, earn.

merito (*adv.*): deservedly.

merus, -a, -um: unmixed, unadulterated, sheer.

metuo, -ere, -ui, -utum (*v.t.* and *i.*): fear.

metus, -ūs (*m.*): fear.

mica, -ae (*f.*): bit, morsel.

minister, -tri (*m.*): servant.

minor, -oris: less, smaller.

minus (*adv.*): less.

mire (*adv.*): wonderfully, extraordinarily.

miror, -ari, -atus (*v.t.*): wonder, marvel at.

mirus, -a, -um: wonderful, astonishing.

miserandus, -a, -um: pitiable.

misere (*adv.*): miserably, desperately.

mitis, -is: gentle.

moderatio, -onis (*f.*): moderation.

moderatus, -a, -um: moderate.

modestia, -ae (*f.*): modesty.

modestus, -a, -um: modest, unassuming.

modo (*adv.*): only.

modus, -i (*m.*): mean, manner.

moenia, -orum (*n. pl.*): town walls.

moles, -is (*f.*): mass, pile.

molestia, -ae (*f.*): annoyance, trouble.

molestus, -a, -um: annoying, irksome.

mollis, -is: soft, delicate.

monachus, -i (*m.*): monk.

monasterium, -ii (*n.*): monastery.

moneta, -ae (*f.*): money, currency.

mons, -tis (*m.*): mountain.

morbidus, -a, -um: diseased, sick.

morbus, -i (*m.*): disease.

mordicus (*adv.*): with the teeth; 'tooth and nail.'

Moria, -ae (*f.*): Folly (Greek: title of a book).

mors, -tis (*f.*): death.

mos, moris (*m.*): custom, habit; *pl.* character.

moveo, -ēre, movi, motum (*v.t.*): move.

mox (*adv.*): soon.

muliercula, -ae (*f.*): woman.

mundus, -i (*m.*): universe, world.

mundus, -a, -um: clean.

munio, -ire, -ii or **-ivi, itum** (*v.t.*): fortify.

musca, -ae (*f.*): fly.

mutatio, -onis (*f.*): alteration, change.

mutilus, -a, -um: mutilated, defective.

muto, -are, -avi, -atum (*v.t.*): change, alter.

nam: for.

nanciscor, -i, nactus (*v.t.*): obtain, get.

naris, -is (*f.*): nostril.

narro, -are, -avi, -atum (*v.t.*): tell, relate.

nascor, -i, natus (*v.i.*): be born, be produced; **natus**: son, of the age of, aged.

nasutus, -a, -um: big-nosed, scornful, censorious.

natu: in age; **natu maximus**: eldest.

naufragium, -ii (*n.*): shipwreck, loss.

nausea, -ae (*f.*): sickness, nausea.

nauseo, -are, -avi, -atum (*v.i.*): be sick.

nauticus, -a, -um: naval, nautical.

navigatio, -onis (*f.*): sailing, voyage.

naviter (*adv.*): zealously.

nebulo, -onis (*m.*): worthless fellow, ruffian.

nedum (*conj.*): still less, not to speak of.

nego, -are, -avi, -atum (*v.t.* and *i.*): deny, say not, refuse.

negotium, -ii (*n.*): business, occupation, pains.

nemo, gen. nullius: no one.

nequaquam (*adv.*): by no means, not at all.

nec, neque: nor, neither, and not.

nervus, -i (*m.*): muscle.

nescioquis, -quid: someone or other, something.

nidor, -oris (*m.*): smell.

nidus, -i (*m.*): nest.

niger, -gra, -grum: black.

nigritudo, -inis (*f.*): blackness.

nihil: nothing; (*adv.*) not at all.

nimirum (*adv.*): without doubt.

nimis, nimium: too much.

nisi (*conj.*): unless, if not, except.

nobilis, -is: well-known; as a noun = noble (coin).

nobilitas, -atis (*f.*): nobility.

nocturnus, -a, -um: of the night, nocturnal.

nolo, nolle, nolui (*v.i.*): be unwilling, refuse.

nomen, -inis (*n.*): name, account.

nomino, -are, -avi, -atum (*v.t.*): name, mention.

nondum (*adv.*): not yet.

nonnihil: something, somewhat.

nonnullus, -a, -um: some, several.

nonnunquam: sometimes.

nosco, -ere, novi, notum (*v.t.*): get to know; **novi** = I know.

nostras, -atis: of our country, native.

novitas, -tatis (f.): strangeness.

novus, -a, -um: new, novel, strange.

nox, noctis (f.): night.

noxius, -a, -um: harmful.

nubes, -is (f.): cloud.

nubilosus, -a, -um: cloudy, foggy.

nubo, -ere, nupsi, nuptum (with dat.): marry (woman as subject).

nudus, -a, -um: naked, bare, exposed, stripped (of money).

nullus, -ius: no one, no.

num (interrog. adv.): whether.

numerus, -i (m.): number.

nunc: now.

nundinae, -arum (f.): market-day, market.

nunquam: never.

nuntio, -are, -avi, -atum (v.t.): announce, tell.

nuper (adv.): recently.

nuto, -are, -avi, -atum (v.i.): nod, totter.

ob (prep. with acc.): on account of.

obambulatio, -onis (f.): walk.

obelus, -i (m.): critical mark on a manuscript.

obeo, -ire, -ii, -itum (v.t.): meet, accomplish.

obicio, -ere, -ieci, -iectum (v.t.): bring up as an objection (see note).

obitus, -ūs (m.): death.

oblectatio, -onis (f.): pleasure.

obnoxius, -a, -um: liable to.

oboleo, -ēre, -ui (v.t. and i.): smell, grow rank or stale.

oborior, -iri, -ortus (v.i.): arise.

obrepo, -ere, -repsi, -reptum (v.i.): steal upon, surprise.

obscurus, -a, -um: obscure.

observandus, -a, -um: reverend.

observo, -are, -avi, -atum (v.t.): pay attention, be attentive.

obsigno, -are, -avi, -atum (v.t.): seal up.

obticesco, -ere, -ticui (v.i.): grow silent.

obtrectatio, -onis (f.): disparagement, detraction.

obtueor, -ēri (v.t.): look at.

obtusus, -a, -um: dull.

obvius, -a, -um: met, encountered.

occasio, -onis (f.): opportunity.

occido, -ere, -cidi, -casum (v.i.): die.

occupo, -are, -avi, -atum (v.t.): seize upon, catch, overtake.

oculatus, -a, -um: far-seeing.

oculus, -i (m.): eye.

odium, -ii (n.): hatred, dislike.

odor, -oris (m.): smell.

oeconomus, -i (m.): steward.

offa, -ae (f.): dumpling.

offendo, -ere, -ndi, -nsum (v.t.): meet with, find, be offensive to, upset.

offero, -ferre, obtuli, oblatum (v.t.): offer.

officialis, -is (m.): secretary.

officina, -ae (f.): workshop.

officio, -ere, -fēci, -fectum (with dat.): hinder, be detrimental to.

officium, -ii (n.): duty, service, office.

oleo, -ēre, -ui (v.t. and i.): smell, smell of.

omitto, -ere, -misi, -missum (v.t.): let go, disregard, pass over.

omnino (*adv.*) : altogether, (not) at all, generally.

onus, -eris (*n.*) : burden.

opera, -ae (*f.*) : work, service, assistance; **operam dare** : devote oneself to; endeavour.

opes, opum (*f.*) : riches.

opinio, -onis (*f.*) : opinion.

opinor, -ari, -atus (*v.i.*) : think, consider.

oppleo, -ēre, -plevi, -pletum (*v.t.*) : fill.

opto, -are, -avi, -atum (*v.t.*) : desire.

opus, -eris (*n.*) : task, work, job.

orbis, -is (*m.*) : globe, earth.

ordo, -inis (*m.*) : rank, order.

ornatus, -a, -um : adorned, equipped.

ornatus, -ūs (*m.*) : dress.

ostendo, -ere, -di, -tum (*v.t.*) : show, display.

ostentum, -i (*n.*) : prodigy, portent.

ostium, -ii (*n.*) : door, entrance.

otium, -ii (*n.*) : leisure, idleness.

paciscor, -i, pactus (*v.i.*) : bargain, come to an agreement.

pacto = modo : aliquo pacto : somehow.

paedor, -oris (*m.*) : stink.

paene (*adv.*) : almost.

pagella, -ae (*f.*) : page of a book.

pallium, -ii (*n.*) : cloak.

palustris, -is : marshy.

panis, -is (*m.*) : bread.

pannus, -i (*m.*) : cloth, garment.

parcus, -a, -um : sparing, moderate.

paries, -etis (*m.*) : wall (of a room).

pario, -ĕre, peperi, partum (*v.t.*) : beget, produce, acquire.

pariter (*adv.*) : together.

paro, -are, -avi, -atum (*v.t.*) : prepare, get ready, obtain.

pars, -tis (*f.*) : part, side.

partim (*adv.*) : partly.

parum (*adv.*) : too little, not enough.

passus, -ūs (*m.*) : pace, step.

pateo, -ēre, -ui (*v.i.*) : lie open, be exposed to.

patior, -i, passus (*v.t.*) : suffer, allow.

patria, -ae (*f.*) : native land.

patrimonium, -ii (*n.*) : inheritance.

pauciloquus, -a, -um : of few words.

pauculi, -orum : few.

paulatim (*adv.*) : gradually.

paulum : a little; **paulo** : by a little, somewhat.

peccatum, -i (*n.*) : sin.

pecco, -are, -avi, -atum (*v.i.*) : sin.

pectus, -oris (*n.*) : chest, breast, heart.

peculiaris, -is : special, peculiar.

pecunia, -ae (*f.*) : money.

pelagus, -i (*n.*) : sea.

pellucidus, -a, -um : transparent.

pendeo, -ēre, pependi (*v.i.*) : hang; depend on.

penes (*prep.* with *acc.*) : in the power of.

penetro, -are, -avi, -atum (*v.t.*) : penetrate, pierce.

penitus (*adv.*) : within, deeply.

pensio, -onis (*f.*) : pension.

pensum, -i (*n.*) : thought, consideration; **nihil pensi habere** : care nothing about.

per (*prep.* with *acc.*) : through, by means of.

percurro, -ere, -curri, -cursum (*v.t.*) : hurry through.

perdisco, -ere, -didici (*v.t.*): learn thoroughly.

perdo, -ere, -didi, -ditum (*v.t.*): lose, destroy.

peregrinatio, -onis (*f.*): foreign travel.

perfero, -ferre, -tuli, -latum (*v.t.*): bring, deliver.

perficio, -ĕre, -feci, -fectum (*v.t.*): complete.

perflabilis, -is: airy, ventilated.

pergo, -ere, perrexi, perrectum (*v.i.*): go, proceed, continue.

periculosus, -a, -um: dangerous.

periculum, -i (*n.*): danger.

perinde (*adv.*): equally; perinde . . . ac: just . . . as.

periodus, -i (*f.*): turn.

peritus, -a, -um: skilful, expert (with *gen.*).

perlego, -ere, -legi, -lectum (*v.t.*): read through.

perlibenter (*adv.*): very willingly.

permitto, -ere, -misi, -missum (with *dat.*): allow.

pernicies, -ei (*f.*): ruin.

perparce (*adv.*): very sparingly, stingily.

perpetuus, -a, -um: continual.

perscribo, -ere, -scripsi, -scriptum (*v.t.*): write fully about, describe in detail.

persequor, -i, -secutus (*v.t.*): follow.

persevero, -are, -avi, -atum (*v.i.*): continue.

persolvo, -ere, -solvi, -solutum (*v.t.*): pay.

perstrepo, -ere, -ui, -itum (*v.i.*): resound, ring.

persuadeo, -ēre, -suasi, -suasum (*v.t.* with *dat.*): persuade, convince.

persuasio, -onis (*f.*): persuasion, argument.

pertinacia, -ae (*f.*): obstinacy, persistency.

pertinax, -acis: persevering, obstinate.

pertraho, -ere, -traxi, -tractum (*v.t.*): drag off, hurry away.

pervado, -ere, -vasi, -vasum (*v.i.*): persevere.

pervenio, -ire, -veni, -ventum (*v.i.*): arrive.

pes, pedis (*m.*): foot.

pestilens, -tis: unhealthy, filthy (of weather).

pestilentia, -ae (*f.*): pestilence, plague.

pestis, -is (*f.*): plague.

peto, -ere, -ii or -ivi, -itum (*v.t.*): aim at, make for, request, attack.

petra, -ae (*f.*): rock, stone.

pharmacopola, -ae (*m.*): apothecary, chemist.

pharmacum, -i (*n.*): drug, medicine.

philosophus, -i (*m.*): philosopher.

pictor, -oris (*m.*): painter.

pictura, -ae (*f.*): painting.

pietas, -tatis (*f.*): piety.

pileus, -i (*m.*): hat.

pilula, -ae (*f.*): pill.

pilus, -i (*m.*): hair.

pingo, -ere, pinxi, pictum (*v.t.*): paint.

piscis, -is (*m.*): fish.

pius, -a, -um: holy, sacred.

placeo, -ēre, -ui, -itum (with *dat.*): to please; mihi placet (*impers.*): I resolve.

plane (*adv.*): quite, entirely.

plenus, -a, -um: full.

pleuritis, -idis (*f.*): pleurisy.

plus, pluris (*neut.* only in *sing.*): more.

pluvia, -ae (*f.*): shower.

pluviola, -ae (*f.*): drizzle.

9

poena, -ae (*f.*): penalty.

poëta, -ae (*m.*): poet.

polleo, -ēre, -ui (*v.i.*): to be strong, powerful.

polliceor, -ēri, pollicitus (*v.t.* and *i.*): promise.

pomeridianus, -a, -um: of the afternoon.

pompa, -ae (*f.*): retinue.

pone (*prep.* with *acc.*): behind.

porrigo, -ere, -rexi, -rectum (*v.t.*): stretch out.

porta, -ae (*f.*): gate.

portendo, -ere, -tendi, -tentum (*v.t.*): portend, presage.

portuosus, -a, -um: rich in harbours.

posco, -ere, poposci (*v.t.*): demand.

post (*prep.* with *acc.* and *adv.*): after, afterwards.

postea (*adv.*): afterwards.

posteaquam (*conj.*): after.

posterum (*sc.* **tempus**): the future.

postremus, -a, -um: last.

postridie (*adv.*): next day.

postulo, -are, -avi, -atum (*v.t.*): demand.

potens, -tis: powerful, influential.

potissimum (*adv.*): preferably.

potius (*adv.*): rather.

prae (*prep.* with *abl.*): in front of, compared with, because of.

praebeo, -ēre, -bui, -bitum (*v.t.*): show, offer.

praecaveo, -ēre, -cavi, -cautum (*v.t.*): take precautions against, guard against.

praecedo, -ere, -cessi, -cessum (*v.t.*): go in front of, excel.

praecello. -ere, no *perf.* (*v.t.* and *i.*): excel, surpass.

praeceptio, -onis (*f.*): instruction.

praeceptor, -oris (*m.*): teacher.

praecipio, -ěre, -cepi, -ceptum (with *dat.*): instruct, order.

praecipito, -are, -avi, -atum (*v.t.*): plunge headlong.

praecipue (*adv.*): especially.

praecordia, -orum (*n.*): stomach, vitals.

praeditus, -a, -um: endowed with.

praedium, -ii (*n.*): estate.

praedo, -onis (*m.*): pirate, robber.

praefatio, -onis (*f.*): preface, title.

praefectus, -i (*m.*): commander.

praefigo, -ere, -fixi, -fixum (*v.t.*): set in front.

praelautus, -a, -um: very sumptuous.

praemoneo, -ēre, -ui, -itum (*v.t.*): forewarn.

praesertim (*adv.*): especially.

praesidium, -ii (*n.*): protection.

praesto, -are, -stiti, -statum or **-stitum** (*v.t.*): show, provide, excel.

Praesul, -is (*m.*): Prelate.

praeter (*prep.* with *acc.*): besides, except, past.

praeterea (*adv.*): moreover.

praetereo, -ire, -ii, -itum (*v.t.*): pass over, omit.

prandeo, -ēre, prandi, *active p.p.* **pransus** (*v.i.*): lunch.

prandium, -ii (*n.*): lunch.

pratum, -i (*n.*): meadow.

precarius, -a, -um: doubtful, obtained by request.

precor, -ari, -atus (*v.t.*): beg, pray.

pretiosus, -a, -um: valuable.

pretium, -ii (*n.*): price, value.

Primas, -atis (*m.*): Primate.

princeps, -ipis (*m.*): leader, prince, chief man.

priusquam (*conj.*) : before.
privatus, -a, -um : private.
pro (*prep.* with *abl.*) : on behalf of, instead of, in proportion to.
probatio, -onis (*f.*) : probation.
probe (*adv.*) : properly.
probitas, -atis (*f.*) : uprightness, honesty.
probo, -are, -avi, -atum (*v.t.*) : approve.
probus, -a, -um : honest, good.
procedo, -ere, -cessi, -cessum (*v.i.*) : go forward.
proceres, -um (*m.*) : leading men.
procul (*adv.*) : at a distance, far.
procurro, -ere, -curri, -cursum (*v.i.*) : run forward.
prodeo, -ire, -ii, -itum (*v.i.*) : come out, appear.
prodo, -ere, -didi, -ditum (*v.t.*) : betray.
profanus, -a, -um : lay (opp. to clerical), secular.
profectio, -onis (*f.*) : departure.
profecto (*adv.*) : certainly.
profero, -ferre, -tuli, -latum (*v.t.*) : bring out, publish, prolong.
professor, -oris (*m.*) : professor.
proficio, -ere, -feci, -fectum (*v.i.*) : make progress, be successful.
profiteor, -eri, -fessus (*v.i.*) : confess, profess.
progredior, -i, -gressus (*v.i.*) : go forward.
proiectus (*p.p.* proicio) : thrown away.
prolixe (*adv.*) : abundantly.
prolixus, -a, -um : long-winded.
promereor, -eri, -itus (*v.t.*) : deserve, gain.
promiscuus, -a, -um : mixed.
promitto, -ere, -misi, -missum (*v.t.*) : promise.

propemodum (*adv.*) : almost.
propendeo, -ere, -di, -sum (*v.i.*) : to be inclined to.
properatio, -onis (*f.*) : hasty departure.
propino, -are, -avi, atum (*v.i.*) : drink a health, revel.
propinquus, -a, -um : near, neighbouring.
propitius, -a, -um : favourable.
propterea (*adv.*) : therefore.
prosequor, -i, -secutus (*v.t.*) : attend, escort, honour.
prosperus, -a, -um : fortunate, favourable.
prospicio, -ere, -spexi, -spectum (*v.t.* and *i.*) : look out.
protinus (*adv.*) : immediately.
proveho, -ere, -vexi, -vectum (*v.t.*) : carry forward, promote, exalt.
provoco, -are, -avi, -atum (*v.t.*) : challenge.
proximus, -a, -um : nearest, next, last.
prudentia, -ae (*f.*) : foresight, widsom.
publicus, -a, -um : public.
pudet, puduit (*impers. vb.*) : it shames.
pudor, -oris (*m.*) : sense of shame.
puella, -ae (*f.*) : girl.
puer, -i (*m.*) : boy.
puerilis, -is : boyish, childish.
pugna, -ae (*f.*) : fight.
pugnus, -i (*m.*) : fist.
pulcher, -chra, -chrum : fair, pretty.
pulchre (*adv.*) : fairly, pretty.
pullulasco, -ere (*v.i.*) : increase.
puls, -tis (*f.*) : porridge, gruel.
pulvis, -eris (*m.*) : dust, powder.
punctum, -i (*n.*) : point, mark of approval.

purgatio, -onis (*f.*): purging, cleansing, Purification.

purgo, -are, -avi, -atum (*v.t.*): purge, cleanse.

puritas, -atis (*f.*): purity.

purpuratus, -i (*m.*): high official of court.

pusillus, -a, -um: petty, insignificant, poor-spirited.

puteo, -ēre (*v.i.*): smell, stink.

puto, -are, -avi, -atum (*v.t.*): think.

quadriga, -ae (*f.*): four-horsed coach.

quadringenti, -ae, -a: four hundred.

qualis, -is: of such a kind; (*interrog.*) of what kind?

qualisqualis, -is: of whatever sort.

quam: than, as, how.

quamlibet (*adv.*): however.

quamprimum (*adv.*): as soon as possible.

quamquam (*conj.*): although.

quamvis (*adv.* and *conj.*): though, however.

quando (*conj.*): because; (*interrog.*) when?

quantulus, -a, -um: how little?

quantumvis (*adv.*): however much.

quantus, -a, -um: as large, how large?

quare: therefore; why?

quassatio, -onis (*f.*): shaking, jolting.

quemadmodum (*adv.*): how.

queo, quivi (*v.i.*): be able.

quia (*conj.*): because.

quid?: what? why?

quidam, quaedam, quoddam: a certain.

quidem (*adv.*): indeed; **ne . . . quidem**: not . . . even.

quies, -etis (*f.*): rest.

quiesco, -ere, quievi, quietum (*v.i.*): be quiet, rest.

quilibet, quaelibet, quodlibet: any (you like).

quippe (*conj.*): since (usually with *rel. pron.*).

quispiam, quaepiam, quippiam: someone, something.

quisquam, quaequam, quicquam: anyone, anything (in a neg. sentence).

quisque, quaeque, quodque: each.

quisquis, quicquid: whoever, whatever.

quivis, quaevis, quodvis: anyone you like.

quo: whither?

quocirca (*adv.*): therefore.

quod (*conj.*): because.

quodsi (*conj.*): but if, and if.

quominus (*conj.*): that not, from (after verbs of preventing).

quoniam (*conj.*): because, since.

quoque (*adv.*): also.

quotidianus, -a, -um: daily.

quotidie: daily.

quoties (*conj.*): whenever.

rapio, -ěre, -ui, -tum (*v.t.*): hurry away.

raptim (*adv.*): hastily.

rarus, -a, -um: rare.

ratio, -onis (*f.*): reason, method, system.

recipio, -ěre, -cepi, -ceptum (*v.t.*): get back, recover, resume.

recoctus, -a, -um: cooked again, rehashed.

recreatio, -onis (*f.*): recreation, convalescence.

recreatus (*p.p.* **recreo**): restored to health.

recte (*adv.*): rightly.

rectus, -a, -um: erect, correct, right.

recurro, -ere, -curri, -cursum (*v.i.*): hurry back, recur.

redamo, -are, -avi, -atum (*v.t.*): return affection.

reddo, -ere, -didi, -ditum (*v.t.*): give back, render, make.

redeo, -ire, -ii, -itum (*v.i.*): go back.

redimo, -ere, -emi, -emptum (*v.t.*): buy back, ransom.

reditio, -onis (*f.*): return.

reditus, -ūs (*m.*): return.

redormisco, -ere, -dormivi (*v.i.*): go to sleep again.

refert, retulit (*v.i.*): it is of importance, it matters.

refrigesco, -ere, -frixi (*v.i.*): grow cold or stale.

regero, -ere, -gessi, -gestum (*v.t.*): cast back, retort, bandy.

regio, -onis (*f.*): district.

regius, -a, -um: royal, of a king.

regno, -are, -avi, -atum (*v.t.* and *i.*): rule.

regnum, -i (*n.*): kingdom, royal power.

relinquo, -ere, -liqui, -lictum (*v.t.*): leave behind, abandon.

reliquiae, -arum (*f.*): remains, refuse.

reliquus, -a, -um: remaining, the rest.

remedium, -ii (*n.*): cure.

remitto, -ere, -misi, -missum (*v.t.*): send back, remit.

renes, -ium (*m.*): kidneys.

renovo, -are, -avi, -atum (*v.t.*): renew.

repente (*adv.*): suddenly.

reperio, -ire, repperi, repertum (*v.t.*): find.

repeto, -ere, -ii or -ivi, -itum (*v.t.*): seek again, make for again.

repono, -ere, -posui, -positum (*v.t.*): replace.

repugno, -are, -avi, -atum (*v.i.*): oppose, resist.

repullulo, -are, -avi (*v.i.*): grow again, break out again.

reputo, -are, -avi, -atum (*v.i.*): reflect, consider.

resignatio, -onis (*f.*): resignation.

resipisco, -ere, -sipivi or -sipui (*v.i.*): come to one's senses.

respublica, -ae (*f.*): state, city.

respondeo, -ēre, -ndi, -nsum (*v.t.*): reply, agree with.

reticeo, -ēre, -ui (*v.t. and i.*): keep silent, conceal, avoid mentioning.

retineo, -ēre, -ui, -tentum (*v.t.*): hold back.

reverendus, -a, -um: venerable, reverend.

revertor, -i, -versus (*v.i.*): return.

revello, -ere, -velli, -vulsum (*v.t.*): tear away.

reviso, -ere, -visi (*v.t.*): revisit.

revoco, -are, -avi, -atum (*v.t.*): recall.

rhinoceros, -otis (*m.*): rhinoceros.

rideo, -ēre, risi, risum (*v.t. and i.*): laugh, laugh at.

ridiculus, -a, -um: absurd.

rima, -ae (*f.*): gap, chink, slit.

rimula, -ae (*f.*): small crack.

risus, -ūs (*m.*): laughter.

ritu (*abl.* of ritus): in the manner of, like (with *gen.*).

robustus, -a, -um: strong, fit.

rogo, -are, -avi, -atum (*v.t.*): ask.

ruina, -ae (*f.*) : downfall, falling building, ruins.

rumpo, -ere, rupi, ruptum (*v.t.*) : break.

rumor, -oris (*m.*) : rumour.

ruo, -ere, rui, rutum (*v.i.*) : tumble down, rush.

rupes, -is (*f.*) : rock, cliff.

rursum, rursus (*adv.*) : again.

rus, ruris (*n.*) : countryside.

rusticitas, -atis (*f.*) : rusticity, primitiveness.

rusticus, -a, -um : of the country, rustic.

sacellum, -i (*n.*) : chapel.

sacer, -cra, -crum : sacred, holy; **sacrum** : Mass.

sacerdos, -dotis (*m.*) : priest.

sacerdotalis, -is : priestly.

sacerdotium, -ii (*n.*) : priest's office, living.

saeculum, -i (*n.*) : century, age.

saepe, saepenumero (*adv.*) : often.

saevio, -ire, -ii, -itum (*v.i.*) : be furious or violent.

saevus, -a, -um : fierce, cruel.

salarium, -ii (*n.*) : salary.

salsamenta, -orum (*n.*) : salt fish.

salsus, -a, -um : salty.

saltem (*adv.*) : at least, at all events.

salubris, -is : healthy.

salus, -utis (*f.*) : safety, welfare.

salutifer, -fera, -ferum : healthy, salubrious.

saluto, -are, -avi, -atum (*v.t.*) : greet.

salveo, -ere (*v.i.*) : be well; **salve** : Greetings!

salvus, -a, -um : safe and sound.

Sanctus, -a : Saint.

sane (*adv.*) : doubtless, of course.

sanus, -a, -um : healthy, sane.

sapio, -ere, -ivi (*v.i.*) : be wise; *pres. partic.* **sapiens** : wise.

sat, satis : enough.

satisfacio, -ere, -feci, -factum (with *dat.*) : satisfy.

satius (*adv.*) : better, fitter.

saxum, -i (*n.*) : stone, rock.

scandalum, -i (*n.*) : offence.

scaphula, -ae (*f.*) : little boat.

scapulare, -is (*n.*) : short cloak (*see note*).

scateo, -ere (*v.i.*) : be full of, abound in.

sceleratus, -a, -um : wicked, criminal.

scelus, -eris (*n.*) : crime, sin.

schedula, -ae (*f.*) : prescription.

schola, -ae (*f.*) : school.

scholium, -ii (*n.*) : gloss, explanatory note.

scilicet (*adv.*) : of course, forsooth.

scintilla, -ae (*f.*) : spark.

scirpus, -i (*m.*) : rush.

scopulus, -i (*m.*) : cliff, crag.

scrinium, -ii (*n.*) : chest, trunk.

scriptum, -i (*n.*) : writing, composition.

scriptura, -ae (*f.*) : writing, passage of Scripture.

scrupulum, -i (*n.*) : uneasiness, scruple.

scurrilis, -is : scurrilous.

secedo, -ere, -cessi, -cessum (*v.i.*) : withdraw.

secessus, -us (*m.*) : retreat, retirement.

secretarius, -ii (*m.*) : secretary.

securus, -a, -um : free from anxiety.

secus, secius (*adv.*) : otherwise.

sedulo (*adv.*) : industriously, zealously.

sellula, -ae (*f.*) : little seat, bench.

semel (*adv.*) : once.

semihora, -ae (*f.*): half-hour.

semivivus, -a, -um: half-alive.

semper (*adv.*): always.

senectus, -tutis (*f.*): old age.

sensus, -ūs (*m.*): feeling, sensation.

sententia, -ae (*f.*): opinion, sentence.

sentina, -ae (*f.*): drain.

sentio, -ire, sensi, sensum (*v.t.*): perceive, feel.

sequor, -i, secutus (*v.t.*): follow.

serenitas, -atis (*f.*): clear sky, fine weather.

serio (*adv.*): seriously.

serius, -a, -um: serious.

sermo, -onis (*m.*): conversation, language.

sero (*adv.*): late.

servio, -ire, -ivi, -itum (with *dat.*): serve, be a slave to.

servo, -are, -avi, -atum (*v.t.*): keep safe, preserve.

servus, -i (*m.*): servant.

sesquihora, -ae (*f.*): hour and a half.

sesquimensis, -is (*m.*): month and a half.

si: if.

sic: so, in such a way.

sicubi (*conj.*): if anywhere.

significo, -are, -avi, -atum (*v.t.*): make known, signify, mean.

signum, -i (*n.*): standard, mark.

silex, -icis (*m.*): flint.

silva, -ae (*f.*): wood, collection, anthology.

similis, -is: like.

simul (*adv.*): at the same time.

simulatque (*conj.*): as soon as.

sincerus, -a, -um: genuine, sincere.

sine (*prep.* with *abl.*): without.

singularis, -is: remarkable.

singuli, -ae, -a: one each; one at a time (opp. to universi).

sinister, -tra, -trum: on the left hand, left.

siquidem (*conj.*): since indeed.

sobrius, -a, -um: sober.

socer, -cri (*m.*): father-in-law.

sodalis, -is (*m.*): friend, companion.

sodalitas, -atis (*m.*): fellowship, company.

sol, solis (*m.*): sun.

soleo, -ēre, solitus sum (*v.i.*): be accustomed.

solidus, -a, -um: solid.

sollicitudo, -inis (*f.*): anxiety.

sollicitus, -a, -um: anxious, worried.

sōlum, -i (*n.*): soil, ground.

sōlum (*adv.*): only.

sōlus, -a, -um: alone.

solvo, -ere, solvi, solutum (*v.t.*): loose, pay.

somnus, -i (*m.*): sleep.

sonitus, -ūs (*m.*): sound.

sono, -are, -ui, -itum (*v.i.*): make a noise, resound.

sorbitiuncula, -ae (*f.*): small drink, posset.

sordes, -ium (*f.*): filth.

sordidus, -a, -um: dirty.

sors, sortis (*f.*): lot, fate.

spargo, -ere, sparsi, sparsum (*v.t.*): scatter, sprinkle.

spatium, -ii (*n.*): space.

species, -ei (*f.*): appearance.

spectaculum, -i (*n.*): sight, spectacle.

specto, -are, -avi, -atum (*v.t.*): look at, face (a certain direction).

speculatorius, -a, -um: for spying.

spero, -are, -avi, -atum (*v.t.*): hope, expect.

spes, -ei (*f.*): hope.

spina, -ae (*f.*): spine.

spiro, -are, -avi, -atum (*v.t.* and *i.*): breathe.

splendidus, -a, -um: magnificent, sumptuous.

spondeo, -ēre, spopondi, sponsum (*v.t.*): promise, pledge.

sponte (*adv.*): of one's own accord.

sputum, -i (*n.*): spittle.

stabilis, -is: fixed, permanent.

status, -ūs (*m.*): standing position.

sterno, -ere, stravi, stratum (*v.t.*): strew, pave.

stimulo, -are, -avi, -atum (*v.t.*): spur on.

sto, stare, steti, statum (*v.i.*): stand.

stomachus, -i (*m.*): stomach, anger, appetite.

stratum, -i (*n.*): blanket.

strenue (*adv.*): vigorously.

studeo, -ēre, -ui (*v.t.* and *i.*): be eager for, care about.

studiosus, -a, -um: eager, studious.

studium, -ii (*n.*): zeal, enthusiasm, study.

stulte (*adv.*): foolishly.

stupeo, -ēre, stupui (*v.i.*): be amazed.

Styx, -gis (*f.*): River Styx.

suadeo, -ēre, suasi, suasum (with *dat.*): urge, advise.

suavis, -is: pleasant.

suaviter (*adv.*): pleasantly.

sub (*prep.* with *acc.* and *abl.*): under, close to, near.

subduco, -ere, -duxi, -ductum (*v.t.*): withdraw.

subinde (*adv.*): from time to time, repeatedly.

subirascor, -i, -iratus (with *dat.*): be annoyed.

subito (*adv.*): suddenly.

subitus, -a, -um: sudden.

sublatus, from tollo.

submolestus, -a, -um: rather troublesome.

subolet mihi (*impers. vb.*): I suspect, get wind of.

subrideo, -ēre, -risi, -risum (*v.i.*): smile.

subsanno, -are, -avi, -atum (*v.i.*): mock, deride.

subveho, -ere, -vexi, -vectum (*v.t.*): bring up, lift up.

subvereor, -ēri, -veritus (*v.i.*): fear slightly, be apprehensive.

succedo, -ere, -cessi, -cessum (*v.i.*): follow after; (*impers.* use) to be successful.

successus, -ūs (*m.*): success.

succurro, -ere, -curri, -cursum (*v.i.*): help (with *dat.*); to come into one's mind.

sudor, -oris (*m.*): sweat, toil.

sufficio, -ěre, -feci, -fectum (*v.t.* and *i.*): substitute, be sufficient.

suffragor, -ari, -atus (*v.i.*): favour, support.

summa, -ae (*f.*: sum, total.

summopere (*adv.*): very greatly.

sumo, -ere, sumpsi, sumptum (*v.t.*): take.

sumptus, -ūs (*m.*): expense.

supellex, -ectilis (*f.*): furniture.

superfluus, -a, -um: superfluous.

supero, -are, -avi, -atum (*v.t.*): surpass, overcome.

superstes, -stitis: surviving.

supersum, -esse, -fui (*v.i.*): survive, be left.

suppedito, -are, -avi, -atum (*v.t.* and *i.*): furnish, supply.

supra (*prep.* with *acc.*): above, beyond, more than; also *adv.*

surdus, -a, -um: deaf.

surgo, -ere, surrexi, -rectum (*v.i.*): get up.

suspicor, -ari, -atus (*v.t.*): suspect.

sustineo, -ēre, -tinui, -tentum (*v.t.*): hold up, maintain.

sycophanta, -ae (*m.*): flatterer, sycophant.

syncope, -is (*f.*): fainting fit.

syngrapha, -ae (*f.*): promissory note, bond.

tabella, tabula, -ae (*f.*): painting.

tabellarius, -ii (*m.*): messenger, letter-carrier.

taceo, -ēre, -ui, -itum (*v.t.* and *i.*): keep silent (about).

tacitus, -a, -um: silent.

taedium, -ii (*n.*): weariness, boredom.

taeter, -tra, -trum: foul, horrid.

talis, -is: such.

tam: so, as.

tamen: nevertheless, yet.

tametsi (*conj.*): although.

tamquam (*adv.*): as if.

tandem (*adv.*): at last.

tango, -ere, tetigi, tactum (*v.t.*): touch, affect.

tantillum (*adv.*): nec tantillum: not in the least.

tantopere (*adv.*): so greatly.

tantulus, -a, -um: so small.

tantum (*adv.*): so much, only.

tantundem (*adv.*): just as much.

tantus, -a, -um: so great.

tectum, -i (*n.*): house, roof.

tego, -ere, texi, tectum (*v.t.*): cover, protect.

telones, -is (*m.*): customs officer.

telonicus, -a, -um: of the customs.

temere (*adv.*): rashly, hastily.

temperies, -ei (*f.*): temperature, temperateness.

tempestas, -atis (*f.*): weather, storm.

tempus, -oris (*n.*): time.

tenaciter (*adv.*): tenaciously.

tenax, -acis: tenacious.

tendo, -ere, tetendi, tentum (*v.t.* and *i.*): stretch, tend, move.

tento, -are, -avi, -atum (*v.t.*): attempt, attack.

tenuis, -is: thin, scanty.

tepidus, -a, -um: tepid, lukewarm.

terrenus, -a, -um: earthen.

terreo, -ēre, -ui, -itum (*v.t.*): frighten.

tessella, -ae (*f.*): window-pane.

testatus, -ūs (*m.*): evidence, proof.

testificor, -ari, -atus (*v.t.*): bear witness to.

testor, -ari, -atus (*v.t.*): bear witness to, testify.

theologia, -ae (*f.*): theology.

theologicus, -a, -um: theological.

theologus, -i (*m.*): theologian.

thus, thuris (*n.*): incense.

timeo, -ēre, -ui (*v.t.*): fear.

titulus, -i (*m.*): title, degree.

tolerabilis, -is: bearable, passable.

tolero, -are, -avi, -atum (*v.t.*): endure.

tollo, -ere, sustuli, sublatum (*v.t.*): raise, remove.

torqueo, -ēre, torsi, tortum (*v.t.*): twist, torture.

tot: so many.

tractabilis, -is: manageable, tractable.

tracto, -are, -avi, -atum (*v.t.*): handle, treat, discuss.

tractus, -ūs (*m.*): district, tract of land, area.

trado, -ere, -didi, -ditum (*v.t.*): hand over.

traduco, -ere, -duxi, -ductum (*v.t.*) : carry over, bring over, translate.

tragico-comedia, -ae (*f.*) : tragi-comedy.

transeo, -ire, -ii, -itum (*v.t.* and *i.*) : cross.

transigo, -ere, -egi, -actum (*v.t.*) : transact.

transmitto, -ere, -misi, -missum (*v.t.*) : send over, hand over.

tremo, -ere, -ui (*v.i.*) : tremble, fear.

tribuo, -ere, -ui, -utum (*v.t.*) : assign, grant.

triduum, -i (*n.*) : three days.

tristis, -is : sad, gloomy.

triumpho, -are, -avi, -atum (*v.i.*) : triumph.

tuba, -ae (*f.*) : trumpet.

tueor, -ēri, tuitus (*v.t.*) : look at, look after, protect.

tum : then; **tum . . . tum** : both . . . and.

tumultuarie (*adv.*) : in haste.

tumultus, -ūs (*m.*) : confusion, riot.

turba, -ae (*f.*) : crowd.

turris, -is (*f.*) : tower.

tutela, -ae (*f.*) : protection, care.

tuto (*adv.*) : safely.

tutor, -oris (*m.*) : guardian.

tutus, -a, -um : safe.

ubi : when, where?

ubicumque : wherever.

ubinam : where?

ubique : everywhere.

ulciscor, -i, ultus (*v.t.*) : avenge, take revenge for.

ulcus, -eris (*n.*) : ulcer.

uliginosus, -a, -um : marshy.

ullus, -a, -um : any.

ulna, -ae (*f.*) : elbow, arm.

ultimus, -a, -um : furthest, last.

ultra (*prep.* with *acc.*) : beyond.

umbra, -ae (*f.*) : shadow.

unde : whence (*rel.* and *interrog.*).

undenam : whence?

unicus, -a, -um : sole, single.

universitas, -tatis (*f.*) : university.

universus, -a, -um : all together.

unquam : ever.

unusquisque, unaquaeque, etc. : each one.

urbs, urbis (*f.*) : city.

usquam : anywhere.

usque : as far as.

usus, -ūs (*m.*) : use.

utcumque (*adv.*) : however, as best one can.

uterque, utraque, utrumque : each of two, both.

utilis, -is : useful, expedient.

utilitas, -atis (*f.*) : usefulness, expediencey.

utinam : would that !

utor, -i, usus (with *abl.*) : use, employ.

utpote (*adv.*) : since, seeing that (with *pres. partic.*).

utrimque (*adv.*) : on or from both sides.

vaco, -are, -avi, -atum (*v.i.*) : have time for, devote oneself to.

valde (*adv.*) : greatly.

valeo, -ēre, valui (*v.i.*) : be powerful, be able.

valetudo, -inis (*f.*) : health (good or bad).

valide (*adv.*) : strongly.

vapor, -oris (*m.*) : vapour.

varius, -a, -um : varied, various.

vas, vasis (*n.*) : vessel, cask.

vectigal, -is (*n.*) : tax.

vehementer (*adv.*): strongly, violently.

veho, -ere, vexi, vectum (*v.t.*): carry; (in *passive*) ride, sail, etc.

vel . . . vel: either or; **vel:** even.

velum, -i (*n.*): curtain.

velut: as if.

venefica, -ae (*f.*): sorceress, witch.

venia, -ae (*f.*): pardon, leave.

venio, -ire, veni, ventum (*v.i.*): come.

venter, -tris (*m.*): stomach, greed.

ventus, -i (*m.*): wind.

verbum, -i (*n.*): word.

vereor, -ēri, veritus (*v.t.*): fear.

versor, -ari, -atus (*v.i.*): live, be engaged in.

vertex, -icis (*m.*): peak.

verto, -ere, verti, versum (*v.t.*): turn, translate, change.

verum: but.

verus, -a, -um: true.

vespertinus, -a, -um: of the evening.

vestio, -ire, -ivi or -ii, -itum (*v.t.*): clothe.

vestis, -is (*f.*): clothing.

vestras, -atis: of your country.

veto, -are, -ui, -itum (*v.t.*): forbid.

vetus, -eris: old.

vexo, -are, -avi, -atum (*v.t.*): worry, harass.

via, -ae (*f.*): way, road.

vibro, -are, -avi, -atum (*v.t.*): shake.

vices (*f. pl.*): changes, vicissitudes.

Vicepraepositus, -i (*m.*): Vice-Provost.

vicinia, -ae (*f.*): neighbourhood.

vicinus, -a, -um: neighbouring, next door, near.

vicissim (*adv.*): in turn.

vicissitudo, -inis (*f.*): changes.

victus, -ūs (*m.*): food.

vicus, -i (*m.*): village.

videlicet (*adv.*): evidently, namely.

vigilans, -tis: watchful.

vigiliae, -arum (*f.*): keeping awake, vigilance.

vinco, -ere, vici, victum (*v.t.*): conquer, surpass.

vindico, -are, -avi, -atum (*v.t.*): claim, punish, avenge.

vindicta, -ae (*f.*): vengeance.

vinolentia, -ae (*f.*): drunkenness.

vinum, -i (*n.*): wine.

violentia, -ae (*f.*): vehemence, violence.

vir, viri (*m.*): man, husband.

virago, -inis (*f.*): female warrior, Amazon.

virulentus, -a, -um: poisonous, virulent.

vis, vim (*f.*): (*sing.*) force, quantity; (*pl.*) strength.

viscum, -i (*n.*): birdlime.

viso, -ere, visi, visum (*v.t.*): visit.

vita, -ae (*f.*): life.

vito, -are, -avi, -atum (*v.t.*): avoid.

vitreus, -a, -um: made of glass.

vivo, -ere, vixi, victum (*v.i.*): live.

vix: scarcely.

vociferor, -ari, -atus (*v.i.*): shout, bawl.

voco, -are, -avi, -atum (*v.t.*): call.

volito, -are, -avi, -atum (*v.i.*): fly.

voluptas, -tatis (*f.*): pleasure.

vomitus, -ūs (*m.*): vomit.
votum, -i (*n.*): prayer, vow.
voveo, -ēre, vovi, votum (*v.t.* and *i.*): make a vow.
vulgaris, -is: common.
vulgatus, -a, -um; common.

vulgus, -i (*n.*): crowd, common people.
vultus, -ūs (*m.*): face, expression.

xenium, -ii (*n.*): present.

ADDENDA

accendo, -ĕre, -cendi, -censum (v.t.) : set on fire.
adeo (adv.) : to such an extent, so.
ambitio, -onis (f.) : ambition.

baro, -onis (m.) : baron.
bis (adv.) : twice.
blande (adv.) : courteously, pleasantly.

celo, -are, -avi, -atum (v.t.) : conceal.
commoror, -ari, -atus (v.i.) : stay.
conviva, -ae (m.) : guest.

defero, -ferre, -tuli, latum (v.t.) : carry.
dependo, -ĕre, -pendi, -pensum (v.t.) : pay.

ebrietas, -tatis (f.) : drunkenness.
elegans, -tis : elegant, charming.
experior, -iri, expertus (v.t.) : experience, encounter.

favor, -oris (m.) : favour.

gladius, -ii (m.) : sword.
gratis (adv.) : frec of charge.

hiems, -is (f) : winter.

ictus, ūs (m) : blow.
inspicio, -ĕre, -spexi, -spectum (v.t.) : look at.

largior, -iri, -itus (v.t.) : bestow.
laus, -dis (f.) : praise.
liberalitas, -tatis (f.) : generosity.
lineus, -a, -um : (made of) linen.

moror, -ari, -atus (v.i.) : delay.

neglego, -ĕre, -lexi, -lectum (v.t.) : neglect, fail.

occido, -ĕre, -cīdi, -cisum (v.t.) : kill.
occulto, -are, -avi, -atum (v.t.) : hide.
omen, ominis (n.) : omen.
opprimo, -ĕre, -pressi, -pressum (v.t.) : crush.

pertineo, -ere, -tinui, -tentum (v.i.) : pertain to.
plusquam (adv.) : more than.
posthabeo, -ere, -habui, -habitum (v.t.) : consider of less importance.
praedico, -are, -avi, -atum (v.t.) : declare.

quondam (adv.) : once.

resto, -are, -avi, -atum (u.i.) : remain.
revalesco, -ĕre, -valui (v.i.) : recover.

sedeo, -ere, sedi, sessum (v.i.) : sit.
sedes, -dis (f.) : home.

tener, -a, -um : tender, weak.
trunco, -are, -avi, -atum (v.t.) : dismember.

unguis, -guis (m.) : nail.

vagor, -ari, -atus (v.i.) : wander.
vigor, -oris (m.) : strength.